ONE GOOD REASON

*A Memoir of
Addiction and Recovery,
Music and Love*

SÉAN MCCANN
WITH ANDREA ARAGON

NIMBUS
PUBLISHING
— NIMBUS.CA —

Nimbus Publishing Limited
3660 Strawberry Hill Street, Halifax, NS, B3K 5A9
(902) 455-4286 nimbus.ca

Printed and bound in Canada
NB1515

Editor: Whitney Moran
Design: Heather Bryan
Cover photo: Megan Vincent
Interior illustrations and hand-lettering: Bee Stanton
All interior photos courtesy of the authors.

Title: One good reason : a memoir of addiction and recovery, music and love / Séan McCann with Andrea Aragon
Names: McCann, Séan, 1967- author. | Aragon, Andrea, author.
Identifiers: Canadiana (print) 20200165585 | Canadiana (ebook) 20200171917 | ISBN 9781771088220 (hardcover) | ISBN 9781771088237 (HTML)
Subjects: LCSH: McCann, Séan, 1967- | LCSH: Musicians—Canada—Biography. | LCSH: Recovering alcoholics—Biography. | LCSH: Adult child sexual abuse victims—Biography. | LCSH: Great Big Sea (Musical group)
Classification: LCC ML420 .M114 A3 2020 | DDC 782.42164092—dc23

 Canada Council for the Arts   Conseil des arts du Canada

Nimbus Publishing acknowledges the financial support for its publishing activities from the Government of Canada, the Canada Council for the Arts, and from the Province of Nova Scotia. We are pleased to work in partnership with the Province of Nova Scotia to develop and promote our creative industries for the benefit of all Nova Scotians.

This story is dedicated to our boys, Keegan and Finnegan:
two good reasons to never give up.

PUBLISHER'S NOTE

This book contains allegations of a criminal act by a person who was never legally prosecuted, and therefore this person is not named herein. In lieu, this person will be referred to as "the priest."

AUTHORS' NOTE

The purpose of this book is not to cast blame or offer excuses. While my battle with addiction was waged across my many years with the band, I take full and sole responsibility for my bad behaviour and any harm or hurt feelings I may have caused. In the end, I am the one who had to change, and I truly believe it was for the good of everyone. I sincerely hope my story brings only healing and recovery, even to those who would rather not hear it.

–Séan

I was never a member of Great Big Sea but I am a founding member of family Aragon-McCann and I know full well the toll addiction can take on a marriage and young children. While I still fight hard for all of us every day, it is not my intention to create any new enemies in this sharing of our truth. I hope these pages lead only to help and never to hurt.

–Andrea

We are made of music and we are made of love.

Fire

Tell me where you're going
Show me where you've been
Open up your heart
And let me in

Tired of never knowing
What you're gonna do
Don't just stand there
Walk right through

I'm gonna walk through the fire
Gonna get a little higher
Gonna let these flames
Lead me to the light

I won't drown my sorrow
In a sea of old tomorrows
I'm gonna walk right through the fire
And take my time
Pride is hard to swallow
And light is hard to follow
Truth is hard to see
When we close our eyes

A man is free to wander
To steal and beg and squander
The love he gets
He cannot understand

Minds are made to wonder
Hearts beat like thunder
But in the flames
I'll find out who I am

PRELUDE

♡

NOVEMBER 9, 2011, is the anniversary of my husband Séan's sobriety. It's an amazing accomplishment and one that helped save our marriage, and our family, but it was also the beginning of a world of hurt I tried not to see coming. On this day, when my husband celebrates, I'm reminded why I had to give him an ultimatum to sober up, to choose us over booze. I'm reminded of the worst day of my life. I'm reminded of the words that literally brought me to my knees.

But a lot happened to us—two broken people—before we found each other. Things that could have torn us apart or crushed us.

While it certainly battered us, we ended up here, in a place of truth, compassion, loyalty, and most of all, love. Together.

This is our story.

PART I

GENESIS

THE LION LIES DOWN WITH THE LAMB

"**F**ORGIVE ME, FATHER, for I have sinned and it's been a week since my last confession. Since then I stole some comics from my brother and I lied to my mom."

"Anything else?"

"No, Father."

"Are you sure?... Have you had any impure thoughts?"

"Father?"

"About girls...?"

"Oh. Yes, Father...sometimes...."

"Do you ever act on these thoughts?"

"No, Father."

"Not even when you are alone...by yourself?"

"Yes, Father...."

"Masturbation is a mortal sin against God and His holy church. We must control our urges or face eternal damnation. Do you understand?"

"Yes, Father."

"Are you sorry?"

"I am, Father."

"Then by the power and the mercy of the Lord Jesus Christ, I absolve you in the name of the Father, the Son, and the Holy Spirit. For your penance, say the rosary every day this week starting with the Sorrowful Mysteries and come back to me for confession next Friday."

"Yes, Father."

"What is your name?"

"...Father?"

"Your name. Who are you?"

"My name is Séan McCann, Father."

"And what grade are you in, Séan?"

"Grade nine, Father."

"And what are you reading?"

"Whatever my teachers tell me to read, Father."

"We shall have to do something about that. You have given me an honest confession, Séan, and I would really like to meet you. Would you please wait for me until I am finished hearing confessions so we can talk some more?"

"Yes, Father. I will."

HOLD ME MOTHER

I WAS BAPTIZED and raised as a devout Catholic. Every Sunday we dressed up in our best clothes and headed off to church, which I always found really boring—except for the singing. I loved to sing and some of the old hymns, like "Lift High The Cross" and "O Come, O Come Emmanuel," were great. The only other enjoyable thing about going to mass was when the priest asked the congregation to "offer each other the sign of peace." This would always trigger a round of vigorous handshaking and well wishes; a chance to look neighbours right in the eye and let them know who you were and what you were made of. I remember having my five-year-old hand almost crushed by full-grown men determined to teach me the value of a strong handshake.

Character builders.

In school we were forced to learn and accept all the teachings of the church. Life's biggest questions: the difference between good and evil, and where we go when we die, we surrendered entirely to the Church's authority and let the promise of faith lead us in our mortal lives. The sin of doubt was always met with the swift application of guilt, an entirely negative emotion used constantly as a means of behavioural control. Jesus was tortured and horrifically murdered because of our sins, so the very least we could do was obey the church he left behind to help us. I spent the better part of my young life believing that I was somehow personally responsible for Christ's crucifixion, and I'm certain my mom and dad suffered from the same complete mindfuck.

The intention of this book is not to make excuses for what happened to me, nor is it to let anyone off the hook (myself included), but I believe that trauma can be felt across generations and I suspect my parents suffered much at the hands of their spiritual shepherds. More, perhaps, than they are willing to admit, even now. I also want to provide some context as to the culture of the day. It won't make me feel any better about what happened. It won't take away my pain. But it might help explain how this evil was able to thrive undetected, or perhaps deliberately ignored, for generations. An insidious culture of indoctrination and power.

Systemic and absolute.

Infallible.

I carried my heavy secret around for thirty years because I was ashamed of myself and afraid to tell my parents what happened. Over time this shame grew into anger and eventually into a sense of immense betrayal. Each year it took more and more booze and drugs to keep my hidden suffering at bay. My dark secret was slowly eating away at me from the inside, like a caged animal trying to get out.

Sometimes a song can help us speak the words that are just too hard to say, and this is how I finally chose to inform my parents about my abuse. When *Help Your Self* was released in January 2014, Mom told me she loved it (as always), but initially made no specific mention of the special song I'd written for her. I remember us sitting alone at the kitchen table one evening after a family dinner when she finally asked the question I had been waiting to answer for thirty-five years.

"Were you ever abused, Séan?"

"Yes, Mom, I was."

"Whatever you do, please don't tell your father."

Hold Me Mother

Hold me mother I've met my match
Show me a family with no strings attached
Hold me mother 'coz I'm out of control
Tell me the story that I need to know

Now I'm a singer in search of a song
To do what is right and to write what is wrong
Out here in the open there's nowhere to hide
So strap yourself in
Let's go for a ride

When I was 15 I met the pope
When I was 16 I met rum and coke
You were so disappointed when I left him behind
To find me a faith that wasn't so blind

But I never found it so back here I am
My heart on my sleeve and a glass in my hand
So tell me a story and make it half true
Was it something I did or I didn't do?

Hold me mother I need some protection
There's cracks in these walls upon closer inspection
The lights have come on now I see things clearly
I know that you're here
But I don't know that you hear me

You give your grandson some rosary beads
He loves you like me but that's not what he needs
He picks up the phone and tells you he's lost
You tell him about someone we nailed to a cross

I never found him so back here I am
My heart on my sleeve and a glass in my hand
So tell me a story and make it half true
Was it something I did or I didn't do?

Hold me mother I need to be guided
I look to the sky and remain undecided
You don't need to be young to be wasting your days
You don't need to be old to be set in your ways

And if you were here now
this is what I would say

SHOW ME A FAMILY

I WAS BORN in the very small town of Carbonear, Conception Bay, Newfoundland, on May 22, 1967. The first child of recently wed Anita March of Northern Bay and Ed McCann of neighbouring Gull Island. The two outports sit "side by each" on the Bay de Verde Peninsula and have supported their minor populations (approximately five hundred combined) for almost three centuries exclusively with the inshore cod fishery. Settled by Irish immigrants fleeing famine and religious persecution, the inhabitants were also exclusively Catholic. My mother's labour was difficult and long, a foreshadowing of our future relationship. My father, who was generally not a drinking man, had time to get drunk twice during the eighteen-hour ordeal. I was a very big baby and I cried loud and often.

I still do.

On my father's side, the McCanns were a hardy fishing family of sixteen who managed to somehow scrape a living off the rocks in "the Gulch," where they lived in exile due to a mixed marriage in a previous generation. While Catholics and Protestants worked side by side out of necessity, they were strictly forbidden from falling in love and the social penalty from both sides was high.

Isolation.

Jeremiah, my grandfather, was a well-respected jack-of-all-trades and did whatever it took to keep his large hungry family fed in the modest four-bedroom saltbox house they called a home. He fished, farmed, hunted, and cut wood. Generally a quiet man, he was known to be good with his fists when it was called for and on several occasions used this skill to secure his berth on treacherous sealing vessels, putting himself at great risk copying (essentially running) over the ice floes in the dangerous pursuit of pelts. This bloody and perilous work provided a desperate infusion of cash and fresh meat in early spring when household larders were at their lowest. "Daddy Jerry," as he was affectionately known by his lawless gang of grandchildren, was a gentle man with giant hands and a glass eye, the result of an accident while playing with dynamite blasting caps as a child. The injury quite likely saved his life, as it prevented him from passing the physical exam when he tried to enlist in the First World War at the age of fifteen. A pipe smoker from the age of ten, he had another close brush with death in his sixties when he developed cancer in his throat and lower lip. There was no real form of treatment at the time so Jerry sought the help of a spiritual healer on the mainland in the small town of Sydney, Cape Breton, where he had sometimes worked as a coal miner. He credited the application of a special bread poultice and the endless repetition of the rosary with saving his life. After a month the malignancy literally fell from his face, leaving him with nothing but a bad facial scar. He was cancer-free. (He would only quit smoking when he was seventy-two because tobacco went up to two dollars a package.) Before he finally left this world, he told me that when he was my age (twenty-one at the time) his life looked like a very long road ahead but now that he was at the end and looking back, he felt like it had all happened in a single blink. He was ninety-eight years old when he died.

Hard as nails.

Jeremiah McCann married Agnes McCarthy of Red Head Cove on December 26, 1917, and the couple proceeded to spend the next sixty-nine years together. Agnes, or "Ma" as everyone called her, was known for her fiery temper and sharp tongue—and who could blame her? She gave birth to sixteen children and outlived almost half.

Ma was a woman of selective beliefs. She considered Neil Armstrong's walk on the moon to be an elaborate US government hoax but never missed an episode of her favourite TV show, *Maple Leaf Wrestling*, which aired every Saturday on one of our two available channels. She was particularly fond of "Macho Man" Randy Savage. Ma was a very proud teetotaller her entire life but took great comfort in her daily medicinal "tonic," which she ordered from the Gerald S. Doyle catalogue and consumed every evening after supper. Its effect was always to make her much more approachable and docile; my inner addict would love to know exactly what that over-the-counter cure was really made of.

When I was just eight years old, I fainted on Ma's front porch after badly cutting my left index finger with a splitting axe. This was back in the days before safety helmets and seat belts, when small boys still played with sharp things. I remember her slapping me hard across the face to wake me and wrapping my mangled finger up with some black electric tape to stop the bleeding. When I questioned her rather rough and rudimentary treatment, her simple response was: "If you scalds your arse, you gotta learn to sit on the blisters."

Salt of the earth.

The Marches of Northern Bay on my mother's side were also Catholic but cut from a slightly finer cloth. The progeny of another mixed faith marriage, in 1863 my great-great uncle John was only the second March on the north shore to be baptized a Catholic (he was preceded a year earlier by his father, Simeon, who converted from the Anglican church so he could marry my Catholic great-great-grandmother, Cecilia). He attended school in Northern Bay until he was fourteen years old and was known to assist his formerly Protestant father with his successful family business: a cod liver oil factory. From his industrious dad, John March acquired the sound principles of order and method which later shone so conspicuously in his storied religious career. In 1882, at the age of eighteen, John felt his spiritual calling (from the Catholic side) and left for Rome, where he received his ordination from the Propaganda College on March 16, 1889. He arrived back in Newfoundland in June of that year, where he was appointed curate at the diocese of Harbour Grace.

For many years John did missionary work in Labrador, harvesting "heathen" souls from the Indigenous peoples who still remembered how to live off the natural bounty of "The Big Land." His star rose quickly within the local ecclesiastical ranks and, much to the chagrin of every Protestant who ever hailed from Conception Bay, on November 4, 1906, he became the first native Newfoundlander to be consecrated bishop of the diocese of Harbour Grace. He was now one of the most wealthy and powerful men in

Britain's newest dominion. (Newfoundland would be granted Dominion status in 1907.)

The Most Reverend John March was, by all accounts, well respected by both the public and his religious peers, so it came as quite a shock when, while saying mass on October 19, 1913, there was a brazen attempt made on his life. It was, understandably, very big news at the time. Here's how the local newspapers described the shocking event:

ATTEMPT ON LIFE OF BISHOP OF HARBOUR GRACE

His Lordship Bishop March was shot at while celebrating Mass on the Cathedral Altar here to-day. One bullet slightly grazed His Lordship's head, the other being found embedded in the plaster.

The would-be assassin is a young Catholic man of this community named James Hare, who recently returned from Sydney, CB. He bore a good reputation previous to leaving here, but it is believed he is now mentally afflicted. He is a hard drinker and also has acquired anarchistic ideas, and is reported to be connected with some association abroad. He says he is a Socialist.

Hare approached the Altar thru the vestry door, entered the chancel and fired the first shot from a seven chamber 22 calibre revolver at His Lordship 12 feet distant. Then he quickly advanced to within six feet and fired the second shot. Several men hurried over the Altar rails, captured the man and took the revolver containing four unfired cartridges. The [sic] removed him to the prison cell in the Court House gaol. Intense excitement prevailed, many of the women fainting, whilst others rushed from the church. The man at first was not recognized and was supposed to be an anarchist.

His Lordship, after seeing the man properly protected from the violence of the excited men, returned to the Altar and continued celebrating Mass. At its conclusion he asked the congregation not to attach any importance to the incident, stating that the poor man was obviously demented and therefore not responsible for his action.

—Excerpted from *The Harbour Grace Standard*, October 19, 1913

～

James Hare, aged about 27, of Harbour Grace, who returned three weeks ago from Sydney, at 10:50 a.m., went in the west door, halted west of the Altar and fired two shots. Bishop March was celebrating Mass and was facing the congregation. One bullet from the revolver grazed the right side of the top of his head making a mark the size of a herring scale. Hare is a member of Bishop March's flock. It is not known if Hare was at the service. He called one day last week and asked the Bishop what he had against him. The Bishop believed then that the man was insane.

[...]

Many females became weak and several fainted and much trouble was experienced by those who now had the man in charge to keep the excited people from committing violence on the man who came so near taking the life of their beloved Bishop. Great credit is due to Mr. Edward Moriarity, one of the first on the scene, for his presence of mind in grabbing the revolver so as his finger came between the hammer and the cartridge, thus preventing the third and perhaps a fatal discharge of the weapon.

[...]

Constable Grouchey E. Moriarty and M. Stapleton jumped over the rails and seized the man. When they took him he said, "It doesn't matter now, my work here is done."

—Excerpted from the Saint John's *Evening Telegram*, October 19, 1913

Bishop John March's stay of execution that fateful day was seen by his flock as nothing short of miraculous and his stock as a holy man went up considerably. James Hare was never criminally charged but would spend the remainder of his life languishing in the St. John's Lunatic Asylum. But was he mentally deranged, as the newspapers and the bishop himself suggested? Or did he have some legitimate reason to be homicidally angry with my great-great uncle? Family legend claims the bishop saved the man from certain death at the hands of his angry followers by offering his assailant forgiveness. The truth, in the aftermath of what must have been a compelling local news event, remains elusive. Perhaps there actually was some history between the two that the bishop used his power and privilege to suppress. Aside from the newspaper articles referenced above, it's as if James Hare never existed.

A ghost.

The bishop would live out his remaining twenty-seven years as a popular clerical celebrity whose name was always on the best guest lists of the St. John's Catholic business elite. During his reign as a local religious rock star, his holiness led a life of relative luxury and excess as he shepherded his faithful but far-lower-incomed flock. In the midst of the Great Depression, he had a splendid summer residence built in his hometown and called it Cherry Hill. The only house on the shore with its own name, Cherry Hill was a mansion by local standards and came fully equipped with a housekeeper: his niece and my great-aunt, May March. May never married but instead devoted her entire life to the service of her holy uncle and inherited the lavish house when the bishop died peacefully on January 12, 1940.

Great-Aunt May had a brother who was also named after the family bishop. John March, my maternal grandfather, worked for the church as a handyman, doing everything from keeping the furnace filled with coal to polishing the bishop's big black Cadillac. He built a small house in the shadow of Cherry Hill, married a local girl named Mary Hogan, and together they raised six children. John and Mary's first-born, my mom's oldest "sister," never really lived with her Northern Bay family. She actually spent her early years living with her loving "aunt" May at "The Palace" in Harbour Grace, only returning to Northern Bay to attend school after the bishop's death in 1940. Strange as it may seem, this arrangement was never questioned by anyone in the family, although it was most certainly the subject of whispers and gossip in the small village.

Was my mother's sister really her first cousin?

The bishop was responsible for the issuance of birth certificates, and as such, possessed the power to suppress the truth. But in this case, did he also create it, to hide another family secret?

The Catholic Church was the primary employer of fully half my family tree for an entire generation and some dark secrets are still not ready to be uncovered.

For the Marches of Northern Bay, religion was more than mere faith; it was the family business. Mom's other sister decided early to carry on the trade and pledged herself to the Sisters of Mercy in St. John's at the age of sixteen. She is now eighty years old and works there still.

For the less educated and financially stable McCanns of Gull Island, it was a constant method of control. Fishing the North Atlantic out of small boats is precarious work, and having God on your side takes on a much deeper meaning when danger is literally your daily bread.

Back in the day, faith played a much bigger role in people's life decisions (or lack thereof). The Church offered power and stability amidst an unpredictable and often tragic existence. Poverty and pain were the constant companions of most Newfoundland families prior to Confederation and the clergy was believed to be the only help for many. Life on earth was hard, but the church held the keys to the gates of paradise for those willing to follow and obey, and for centuries, through ignorance and inexplicable hardship, we did.

My father was the second youngest of sixteen brothers and sisters and his young life saw no shortage of severe tragedy. When he was just nine years old he suffered the traumatic loss of two older brothers, Pat (or "Pad," seventeen) and Dan (fifteen), on the same day when they both fell through the ice and drowned while skating on Gull Island Pond. Pad was a strapping young man, strong and fierce and full of life. Dan was gentler and more cerebral and was Dad's closest friend in the world. Apparently Dan fell through the ice first and Pad skated across the pond and jumped into the freezing water to rescue him. Everyone else on the pond that day, men and boys alike, was so frightened they all ran away. If anyone had tried to do anything to help, one or both boys might have survived. Pad was said to have been still living when his remaining brothers finally went back and hauled him out of the frigid pond, but breathed his last as they rolled his frozen body over a barrel to rid his lungs of water. The two boys were eventually carried home on a horse-drawn sled and laid out to wake side by side in the kitchen.

The family was gutted. My grandmother was so stricken by grief and depression she couldn't get out of bed for an entire year. Dad, an altar boy at the time, was shocked by the cold indifference of the local monsignor, Edward O'Brien, who, before entering their bereft home, simply extended his leg and waited for my father to remove his dirty slush-covered galoshes. The two young brothers were laid to rest together in a frozen grave during a raging blizzard. That bitter day never left my father and the emotional trauma would continue to haunt him for his entire life. Though I often asked, Dad would never permit me to serve as an altar boy.

Edward Patrick McCann and Mary Anita March were born within two miles and two years of each other in the neighbouring outport hamlets of Gull Island and Northern Bay and literally grew up together. My father says he always knew he would marry my mother and claims he deliberately failed grade two so they could be in the same class. Aside from a brief one-year break when Mom studied to be a teacher at Littledale College in St. John's, they were always together. It came as no surprise when they were married by Monsignor O'Brien at Corpus Christi Church in Northern Bay on July 2, 1966.

I showed up, as expected, ten and a half months later, and was followed just ten months after that by my baby brother, Glenn. My parents were devout Catholics which meant birth control was entirely in the hands of the Lord; I guess Jesus felt Mom could handle giving birth twice in a year. Burdened with the physical, mental, and financial stresses of a very quickly growing young family, my parents decided to move to the big city of St. John's where there were considerably more employment opportunities. Mom used her connections through her sister at Our Lady of Mercy Convent to secure a teaching job and proceeded to complete her education degree by taking university courses at night. My father got involved in politics and, after successfuly campaign-managing a long-shot candidate, was rewarded for his considerable efforts with a cherished government job. These early days were stressful and challenging for our young family, but my parents both worked extremely hard to keep it all together and I like to believe my own work ethic was genetically inherited.

❧

MY FIRST MEMORY of my mom is of her singing me to sleep.

> In a cabin, in a wood,
> a little man by the chimney stood
> Saw a rabbit hopping by, knocking at the door
> Help me, Help me, Help me, he said
> Before the hunter shoots me dead
> Come on in and stay awhile
> Safe with me abide

I must've been only about three years old, but I distinctly remember the soothing sound of her voice as she sang me and my brother, Glenn, this slightly discomfiting song. She used a series of accompanying hand gestures and I remember being annoyed by Glenn, who was always right there next to me in the crib and kept reaching up to grab her fingers as she sang. If Mom couldn't bring her hands together in the shape of a roof at the end, I was afraid the rabbit wouldn't make it. A lullaby loaded with the lessons of life and death.

My mom was, and still is, an excellent cook. Our house often smelled of fresh homemade bread and my friends were always envious of the excellent sandwiches I brought to school for lunch. But it's still her singing I remember most.

My dad sang a lot too, but it was a much more Buddy Holly and Everly Brothers–based repertoire. He didn't have to spend all his time looking after us and seemed genuinely excited to see us when he got home every day for supper. Dad was a true "bayman" (a Newfoundlander born outside the city-state of St. John's) and his new office gear was a real burden for him. As soon as he got in the front door he would tear off his shirt and tie and chase us all over the house. If he tickled us too much we would pee our pants, which always made mom mad. When supper was called, we all took our shirts off and sat at the table bare-chested, much to my mother's chagrin. Dad's excuse was that he didn't want to get his work shirts dirty. My brother and I just wanted to be like our dad.

My parents were moderate social drinkers. To this day, I have never seen either of them drunk. They were both excellent dancers and occasionally would even break into a 1950s rock 'n' roll jive and swing each other recklessly around the kitchen. It looked a little bit dangerous and it showed me that they, too, were once young like me.

I very seldom saw my parents fight. They always seemed to me to be very much in love.

AMERICAN WOMAN

♡

MY PARENTS COULD not have come from more different backgrounds. Mom comes from an upper-middle class, WASPy family flavoured with southern Italian from her father's side. My dad is a son of migrant workers, Juan and Beatrice Aragon, and grew up very, very poor. His heritage is Mexican/Native American (Beatrice) and Spanish (Juan). His first language is Spanish and he is as brown as any "wetback," the not-so-subtle slur he was subjected to daily by his classmates.

When Juan was eight years old, he was pulled out of school to help provide for his family. As he grew, he held whatever job afforded him any meagre pay to help the family survive. He was everything from a bronco buster (the person who gets on wild, bucking horses to tame them for domesticity) to a sheep herder, to a field worker picking fruit or vegetables on a farm, to a coal miner—when he was old enough. Later in his life, he landed a job at Hill Air Force Base in Utah as a bearing washer. My grandfather used to say to us as young children: "Always do the best you can in whatever job you have, no matter how small it may be. That way you can take pride in knowing you gave your all to the job." He was a very hard-working, humble man who loved gardening and was able to feed his family of six with the literal fruits of his labour. The "lucrative" job at Hill AFB led him to move his family from the Four Corners area of Colorado to Ogden, Utah, with his wife, my dad (five at the time), his two brothers, and his sister in tow. This is where my father would eventually meet my mother, in elementary school. He was poor, and he was brown, when most of Utah was very white.

Mom was expected to graduate high school, become a secretary (or bookkeeper), then get married and start a family. Dad was supposed to work as soon as he could be paid for it—which, it turns out, was about six years old in the fields. The only expectation put on him was to help provide for his family.

My mom ended up pretty much fulfilling her predetermined role by working as a bookkeeper after high school graduation. She was married to my father by the time she was twenty-two. Any ideas of attending college were swept aside, as was expected, in order to get married and raise a family. It was only when I was in high school that my mom got her bachelor's then her master's degree in business, graduating with honours. It's not lost on me that she clearly put her goals on hold as a young woman for the "good" of her husband—and the goal of having a family. When my dad began his business, she ended up working for him as a bookkeeper. One of the most flagrant affairs my dad ever had was with the sister of the receptionist he employed. When asked about their marriage, Mom still says she loved my dad until the day he left the house.

My dad graduated high school and, seeing that he was most likely going to be drafted, enlisted in the army. He was sent to Vietnam when he was nineteen. After one tour, he went back to Utah and, after only being home a few months, married my mom and before promptly moving with her to Fort Ord in Monterey Bay, California, to finish out his enlistment. He graduated with a bachelor's degree in psychology, followed by a master's in business within four years of being discharged. My sister was born while he was in final exams for the latter degree. My mother's attention to their young family allowed my dad the time to focus solely on getting his degrees and starting a business. His free time was mostly spent drinking, smoking dope, and working on his burgeoning business. All of this occurred hundreds of mental miles away from my mom and my sister.

Even though going to church when we visited my dad's parents was pretty standard, I didn't ever think of them as fanatical or strict Catholics. The one time we got on our knees to kiss my grandmother's and grandfather's rings wasn't necessarily a nod to the pope, but more a demonstration of our deference to my dad's parents. For me it was strange; I threw up in my mouth a little as we did it. I hated kneeling before them, hated kissing their rings, but I did not dare cross my dad for fear of "disrespecting" him and being subjected to his volatile temper.

My dad's temper. It was a fifth wheel in our family's carload of crazy. Like a relative who pops in unexpectedly and doesn't say when they're going to leave, my dad's temper took up the figurative basement apartment in our home and we never knew when it was going to come out from its hidey-hole. While I was able to understand later in life how my dad's drinking affected his moods, at this point I was too naive to see this relationship taking root. Although beer (and sometimes stronger liquor) was a constant at our social functions, I was far too self-absorbed during my preteen years to notice how his consumption impacted his moods.

Disrespect seemed to be the biggest trigger for my father's anger as far as I was concerned, though I can't ever remember "disrespecting" him so heinously that it warranted his frightening and soul-crushing outbursts. One time my sister, Jamie, said something snarky at the dinner table (as most preteens do) that led him to rip a piece of bread she was about to eat out of her hand, throw it across the table, and come flying at her from his seat. I thought he was going to either hit her or grab her and throw her. But he never touched her. He just got really close to her face and yelled at her. For Jamie's part—and I was amazed at her courage—she sat stock-still and didn't move a muscle, and looked him straight in the eye. Once he was done yelling at her and sat back down, she continued eating and ignoring us until dinner was done.

Another fun family moment with Anger was at my niece's baptism. I honestly couldn't tell you what I did or what my dad thought I did, but he sat next to me and proceeded to speak to me with such vitriol it brought me to tears. He was chiding me about some phantom misstep I was making while watching my other niece, but I distinctly remember thinking how unprovoked his sneak attack was. Usually I could steel myself for the impending explosion but this had come seemingly out of nowhere. Unfortunately it was always like that with my dad growing up. You never knew when you might be the victim of his caustic tongue.

My dad's mom, Beatrice, was a piece of work in her own way. She was a hard, harsh woman and was verbally abusive to my dad almost always.

I don't remember her ever showing an ounce of affection towards him. She cooked like a motherfucker, though, and would always have amazing food for us when we visited. Homemade bread and rolls (made with lard!), pinto beans, tortillas, chili made with fresh peppers from the garden—her kitchen always smelled like love. It was the only part of her tiny house that elicited that emotion in me.

Grandpa Aragon (Juan) was a sweet, affable man who always let us sit on his knee and made us laugh with his silly Spanish songs. He was an amazing gardener and could grow almost anything. I adored him. He died when I was ten, at the age of eighty-one. It was the first open-casket funeral I had ever been to—the first funeral I had ever been to, period. It was full of ritual, pomp, and incense. My dad made my sister and I go up and kiss my dead grandfather's forehead. Even now, as a forty-seven-year-old woman, the idea of it sickens me. The ten-year-old in me was terrified, but I was more terrified of my father, so I did it.

My dad terrorized the respect right into me throughout my childhood. He demanded it unequivocally, regardless of his own (usually) disrespect-ful attitude and behaviour. It is one of my greatest resentments about our early relationship.

According to my father, matriarch Bonomo was a beast of a woman who constantly berated and belittled her daughter (my mom). She very clearly wore the pants in the family and made no bones about what her desires were or making sure they were met. One of those desires was for my mom to marry. My dad was good enough, and it was inconsequential that, A) he had just returned from war and, B) they didn't actually love each other. Norma Bonomo planned the entire wedding.

I don't remember my mom's parents being particularly loving peo-ple, and memories of dinners at their house in Utah evoke in me no more than a yawn. My last correspondence with them was when they sent me twenty dollars for my college graduation. At one of the last dinners I ever sat with them, they spent the entire time telling me and my sister what a horrible human my father was and how they wished he'd never married their daughter (this was pretty soon after my parents' divorce). Enough said.

According to my mom, her parents were great and nothing bad or unsavory ever happened in their house. Uh-huh. My mom has made "everything is fine" an art form. I have no doubt she learned this from her own mother. This is the house my mom grew up in, and because of it I can't blame her for all of her serious flaws as a parent. (That little nugget took years of self-help and therapy to realize.)

It was only last year, when a dear friend pointed this out to me, that I realized something that changed my life: growing up, I had been learning tacit sufferance; I had been learning how to *be with* an alcoholic. I realized how my tolerance of my father's drinking had been preparing me for my soon-to-be husband, Séan. It was then that I began to see not only my dad's alcoholic patterns, but my role in both these men's addictions. I'd never actually thought of my father as an alcoholic until those words were said to me. I guess we daughters do indeed marry our fathers in one form or another.

ACT OF CONTRITION

"Forgive me, Father, for I have sinned...."

THE SACRAMENT OF Reconciliation is intended to be a private and anonymous exchange between the priest and the penitent. As Catholics, we are taught from birth that we are all born into the original sin of Adam and Eve—the very first crime, carrying severe intergenerational consequences—and that the sins we will inevitably commit here on earth will eventually land us all in hell if we don't come clean. Confession, the baring of one's soul before God's priest, was the Church's remedy for eternal damnation and the only way through the gates of heaven. The Catholic church has many rules surrounding the Holy Sacrament, one being that you can't receive Holy Communion (the risen body and blood of the Lord Jesus Christ) without first being in a state of grace (sin-free). To that end, every Friday students in Newfoundland Catholic schools were strongly encouraged (forced) to spill their guts to the holy priests in the little black boxes that lined the sides of our churches. While our sins remained secret, the event was communal, so we could all surmise how bad our friends had been by how long they were kept in the box and how many prayers they were forced to say afterwards. Public judgement was always swift and cruel for those very few who occasionally found the courage to resist the sacrament.

Low whispers and dirty looks.

Mercy would be found only in the hands of the Lord.

In hindsight, the priest's request to meet me face to face that September day in 1982 should have given me pause. An obvious red flag by today's standards. But at the time I truly believed that a priest was God's representative on earth and ordained with divine power; a holy shepherd sent to care for the Almighty's sheep. I was still just a lamb, so instead of feeling cautious or alarmed, I felt special because Jesus was taking a personal interest in me.

This priest was much younger than the other ancient, slow-moving clerics we were usually subjected to every Sunday. He wore an unruly shock of curly brown hair that bobbed loosely above a long, aquiline nose when he strutted around the church grounds. His legs were short and his arms were long and his eyes were green flashes of madness above a thin-lipped, self-assured grin. Dark lights betraying an inner chaos. Attractive and conflicted. He had bad teeth and his breath smelled of coffee and tobacco.

I waited until the priest finished hearing confessions, and then I took a walk with him around the church grounds. He asked me a lot of questions: What music did I listen to? What kind of books did I read? What did my mom and dad do and where did we live? I tried my best to sound smart and mature. I was only fifteen years old so I wasn't much of either, but he was the most powerful person I'd ever met and I was both terribly intimidated and thoroughly charmed. Up until this point in my brief existence, no adult other than my parents had ever given me this much attention. He talked to me like I was a grown-up and that made me feel like one, which made my confidence swell. He asked me if I prayed to the Virgin Mary. I lied and told him I did, so he invited me to join his new prayer chapter of The Legion of Mary, a voluntary lay organization within the Catholic church devoted to praying to the Virgin Mary—and in this case, a group of kids who met once a week to say the rosary during lunch break at school.

Truth was, I was far more interested at the time in girls who weren't virgins, even though I was still a virgin myself. I agreed to be at the next meeting and went home and asked my mom and dad what the rosary was. This was the first religious instruction I had ever sought from my parents and they were happy to help me get my Hail Mary chops down. They were very curious to know how their son, whose conversation for the past five years had been exclusively devoted to Bobby Orr and his Boston Bruins, had suddenly found his higher spiritual calling. I told them about the new priest and the interest he'd taken in me.

Child protection is a parent's prime directive, but the priest's obvious violation of the confessional rules failed to raise any red flags for them. They asked me to invite my new friend over for dinner after mass on Sunday and when he accepted my invitation, my whole family felt special.

Within a few weeks, the charismatic young priest had completely charmed us all. Dad gave him his own key to our house so he could come and go as he pleased. He visited often and we always bent over backwards to make him feel like one of the family. The first thing he always did when he arrived was take off his uniform (mandatory black shirt and white clerical collar) and change into more casual civilian attire. After meals, he and I would usually engage in horseplay and wrestling in the rec room downstairs. Another sign that went completely undetected by eyes blinded by indoctrination and faith. My parents had opened the door to the lion but all they could see was the lamb.

The priest was the estranged son of a devout Anglican minister from Lewisporte, a small deepwater shipping port of about three thousand souls in Burnt Bay, Newfoundland, connecting the northern coast with the rest of the island by sea. Highly intelligent and extremely charismatic, his religious conversion and fervent embrace of Catholicism could be considered an act of open rebellion against his father and everything else he deemed heretical in the world (and there was much). Completely intolerant of other faiths and prone to saying mass entirely in Latin (he was fluent in four languages), the priest could fairly be described as a radical Catholic fundamentalist. A gifted orator, his zealous dogmatic sermons on theology were always fun to watch even if the subject matter was often miles above the heads of his flock.

Ultra-conservative, he always wore a long black cassock in public to fend off evil, which was everywhere, and perhaps draw more attention to himself. Contraception, divorce, and sex before marriage were all hell-worthy offences without penitential remorse and divine forgiveness. Abortion and homosexuality were completely beyond redemption and the pope was always right. He was emotionally volatile and prone to angry outbursts from the pulpit, often slinging guilt at sinners who, by refusing to come to confession, to the eternal flames of hell were most definitely doomed.

He believed in the literal transubstantiation of the mass (that the sacramental bread and wine literally became the physical blood and body of the risen Jesus Christ) and would throw you out of the church if he caught you accepting the holy Eucharist with gum in your mouth. He was an irritable, unstable genius subject to sudden and violent mood swings. He was thirty-three years old when he entered our lives, "the same age our Lord and Saviour gave his life to save us," he liked to remind us.

He despised modern music (everything created after the Second World War) and insisted I listen to "serious" classical music, which he proceeded to force-feed me on a weekly basis. By fifteen, music was already becoming a passion and I had amassed a considerable collection of classic rock 'n' roll albums which he would often try to steal from my bedroom and destroy. He once ran off with my copy of Pink Floyd's *The Wall* and bought it back to me the next day full of bullet holes.

"Evil music. An abomination."

I learned to hide away my favourite records whenever I knew he was coming over.

He also introduced me to the deeply conservative Christian writers C. S. Lewis, G. K. Chesterton, and Hilaire Belloc, all three of whom I found mostly incomprehensible. But I kept reading to keep him happy. As a gift, he gave me an antique leather-bound edition of Father Alban Butler's Catholic classic, *Butler's Lives of the Saints,* essentially an encyclopedic almanac of the church's accumulated canonizations over the centuries, comprised of several volumes. A different holy role model for me to follow every single day of the year.

The priest was also a great admirer of the British comedian Peter Sellers and we spent many afternoons watching rented VHS copies of his Pink Panther films in my family's rec room, after which we would often re-enact the hilarious combat scenes. These movies became such a preoccupation that I would often hide in waiting like the loyal manservant Cato to ambush my Chief Inspector Clouseau whenever I knew the priest was on his way to our house. My mother would be beside herself when she saw the mess we'd made while rolling around on the basement carpet. Shirts ripped off, faces red, and bodies sweaty from competition. Our relationship got physical very early and we were often left alone. In retrospect, this horseplay was an obvious attempt to make our relationship appear innocent as he groomed me for future sexual contact.

I was the best "friend" he had.

❧

BY THE END of grade nine, the priest had become my constant daily companion. One of our favourite pastimes was to drive his fancy European sports car out to Cape Spear at night and scamper down the rocks to light fires on the beach. A headland on the Avalon Peninsula, Cape Spear is the continent's easternmost point, and while it's popular with tourists, Parks Canada describes the terrain as "treacherous." Locals know it as a dangerous place associated with rogue waves and multiple drownings. On more than one occasion, I saw our fire disappear before my eyes with a loud hiss as the freezing salty foam soaked me suddenly to the bones and sent us clamoring back up the cliff in the slippery ink of a starless night. He always brought his .22 calibre rifle along to shoot at the many plastic bottles and tin cans that washed up on the icy rocks. It was an illegal weapon. Light, low recoil, lethal up to one hundred yards, and fun to shoot—especially after a full bottle of wine when you're in grade nine. He always drove well above the speed limit and we were pulled over on several occasions, but his white collar spared him from anything more than a warning. The clergy in St. John's always got a pass from the Royal Newfoundland Constabulary. I don't remember ever feeling particularly unsafe, but looking back now, I often wonder how we weren't killed while blazing, half lit, down the Cape Spear highway on a foggy night.

Living on the edge and breaking the rules was very exciting for my fifteen-year-old self, and association with the eccentric cleric corresponded to a notable rise in my own popularity at school. Teachers began to see me as the future priest everyone now expected I would become. As the son of a strict elementary school teacher, I'd often been the target of bullying from larger boys with lesser minds. The bullies of Blue River (a small lagoon behind our school where students went to get high) would now let me pass through on my way to class entirely un-tormented. Rumours of my sudden religious conversion made all the pretty girls determined to test my new-found faith with the promise of French kisses and first feels.

Forbidden fruit.

At Halloween that year, the priest let me wear his long black cassock to school as a costume. I cut two holes in a white pillowcase and covered my head so no one could see my hair and face and I roamed the halls, randomly making the sign of the cross as people passed me by. The priest and I were about the same height, so everyone believed I was actually him and automatically paused and bowed their heads to accept my blessings. Even the teachers were quick to pay their respects. I learned that day what it felt like to wield real power over people. I was like a young Luke Skywalker feeling the Force flow through him for the first time. A Hollywood movie star making my way down a high-school red carpet. All eyes were on me and the effect was intoxicating.

Addictive.

Up until this point I had given little real thought to my spiritual vocation, but having literally walked a mile in my mentor's shoes I began to believe my own hype and accept the possibility that I did indeed have a higher calling. Priests had power over people and power was cool...and I wanted to be cool. Perhaps the priesthood could also be my path. I started to dig deeper into the ancient Articles of the Faith and pray daily to the Virgin Mary for guidance and strength. I became fluent in the mysteries of the rosary—The Sorrowful, The Joyful, and the Glorious—and spent many nights on my knees reciting aloud prayers to the Virgin Mother of God.

> Hail Mary full of grace,
> the Lord is with thee.
> Blessed art thou amongst women,
> and blessed is the fruit of thy womb, Jesus.
> Holy Mary, Mother of God,
> pray for us sinners
> now, and at the hour of our death.
> Amen.

These words were repeated fifty times. One prayer for every bead on the rosary chain.

In an effort to impress my new best friend, I enlisted in the church choir and learned to sing in harmony. Aside from the director's son, who played organ, the choir was made up entirely of teenage girls, and my thoughts were often conflicted by corporeal desires as I lifted my voice up to heaven. We wore white robes which covered the shapes of the girls' beautiful young bodies but in the middle of mass my mind would often imagine them singing naked, which only served to fan the flames of my new devotion and lift the zipper beneath my belt. The church was a confusing mixture of power and lust that tickled my burgeoning adolescent sexuality and seduced my teenaged soul. I became a true believer and I wanted to be more.

🦋

IN THE SPRING of 1983 my new "social club," the Newfoundland Legion of Mary, was tasked with making a pilgrimage to the shrine of Sainte-Anne-de-Beaupré. This would require a thirty-hour drive from St. John's to Quebec City, and despite repeated exhortations from the priest, I initially refused until he introduced me to one of the girls who would be in the van. Margaret was two years my senior. She was not so much stunningly beautiful as she was desperately lonely and, to my young romantic mind, readily available. We hit it off over the glorious mysteries and I decided I would go—on the condition that I could sit right next to her.

There were eight other kids willing to make the journey, so the seats were removed from the van to fit us all in. The floor was covered in pillows and blankets and we passed the miles singing hymns and repeatedly saying the rosary. In lieu of seat belts, we placed our trust in Our Lady to save us in the event of an accident. Between mysteries we held hands, and even managed to sneak a few occasional kisses in spite of the tight and uncomfortable conditions.

The driver of the overcrowded holy roller was Margaret's father. George was from Newfoundland's Codroy Valley, a scenic, pastoral collection of small communities on the island's southwest coast. He was a simple farmer and a complete religious fanatic. He dressed like a G-man from the Cold War era and his cockpit dashboard was covered with crucifixes, miraculous medals, statues of saints, and various other religious paraphernalia to help protect him from Lucifer the devil, whom we could occasionally hear him address directly from the back of the van. George saw demons everywhere and spent much of his time verbally casting them out with prayer. He kept one hand on the Bible and the other on the wheel, and he drove as fast as his Ford Econoline could go. Perhaps his distraction is what prevented him from seeing the growing physical attraction between me and his daughter. In retrospect, the real miracle was how we ever survived the long drive with this raving lunatic at the wheel.

Saint Anne was the mother of the immaculately conceived Virgin Mary, making her the second woman in the same family to be impregnated by God. There have been no actual miracles attributed to Anne but I guess as part of Jesus's extended human family she was literally "grandmothered" into her current canonical status. She is known as the divine patroness of unmarried women, housewives, women in labour or who want to be pregnant, grandmothers, educators, and teachers. According to Catholic legend, Anne married a total of three times in her life and is credited with giving birth to two more Marys (for a total of three) and a son. She lived to be fifty-six and is believed to have died in her first daughter's arms with eight-year-old grandson Jesus at her side. In lieu of a standard burial, she was apparently cut into several small pieces and spread across the known world for future veneration. The shrine in Beaupré claims to possess three of her holy bones.

I remember very little about the actual shrine in Sainte-Anne-de-Beaupré. We didn't linger long, because by the time we arrived our driver had received word from our spiritual leader (who had wisely opted to remain at home) that we had been invited to meet with another fervently Catholic lay organization in Montreal called Opus Dei, an elite and secretive ultra-conservative sect within the church. In retrospect, I now believe this was the priest's real plan all along, and that he deliberately didn't tell us in order to avoid potential resistance from parents.

Opus Dei was founded by Father (now Saint) Josemaría Escrivá de Balaguer, on October 2, 1928, in Madrid, when Father Escrivá claimed he experienced a divine vision of "people of every nation and race, of every age and culture, seeking and finding God right in the middle of their ordinary life, their work, their family, their friendships." This inspired him to form "Opus Dei," which in Latin means "Work of God." The group is known for its enthusiasm for the ritualistic practice of corporal mortification, including self-flagellation with five-tailed whips and the painful medieval practice of wearing a cilicios, a sharp, pointed chain worn around the thigh that digs into the flesh.

One of Opus Dei's most prominent supporters was Pope John Paul II, who in 1982 granted the organization special status and increased legitimacy as a personal prelature, which meant that Opus Dei was officially recognized as part of the church's structure. To this day, it remains the only personal prelature under the Vatican.

Montreal was another three hours' drive west and would mean adding an extra day to our already ridiculously long drive home, so this news did not go over well in the back of the van. The decision was not up for debate, however, and George, excited at the prospect of joining yet another religious society, put the van in high gear and headed for new holy ground.

The next morning we met a young Spanish-speaking man named Richard at St. Joseph's Oratory on Mount Royal. He was well groomed and sharply dressed and looked more like a Bay Street lawyer than a religious man. He got right down to business and proceeded to give us all the thirty-minute Opus Dei elevator pitch. I was exhausted and dirty and just wanted to go home. I don't remember much about his speech but did notice an air of disappointment in his voice as it came to an end and he finally bade us goodbye. By now our road-weary group must have looked pretty wretched and I suspect we failed to live up to Richard's expectations. We had driven two thousand kilometres just to be blown off by a holy fucking snob.

We slept that night at a shitty hotel on Crescent Street right next door to a strip joint called La Cave du Sexe. We were four to a room but the sexes were segregated, so fair Margaret wasn't in mine. The next morning, we began the thirty-three-hour slog back to St. John's, and it was as bitter as it was boring. My patience with George and the mental demons that haunted him had worn thin and I was ready to be back in my own bed. When I was finally dropped off at my home in St. John's, I said goodbye to my pilgrim girlfriend and never laid eyes on her again.

The priest was a huge fan of Pope John Paul II and it is my belief that by sending us all off on a crazy deadhead to Montreal he was trying to endear himself to the ranks of the quickly rising and controversial new religious order. Opus Dei was obviously unimpressed with the priest's meagre offering, however, and when we returned to Newfoundland his disappointment was keenly felt at the weekly Legion of Mary meetings. We were now routinely expected to participate in marathon rosary sessions that went on for hours and numbed our young knees. It was nothing short of corporal punishment. We had logged the miracle miles but ultimately failed our holy leader, and he was pissed.

I would like to point out that up until this point I was still a very faithful and practising Catholic. I believed in God and felt he had some kind of special plan for me. I believed his son, Jesus, had died and risen from the dead to save us all. I felt I had a very close and personal relationship with his mother, the Virgin Mary, whom I now spoke to on a daily basis. I believed she was real and took great comfort in sharing my deepest fears and secrets with her. I grew to love her as another mother and trusted her to lead me to my true vocation, and at that time the priesthood was definitely on the table. I never felt as close to Jesus in the same way but figured I didn't have to as long as I had his mom on my side.

My whole life I had been trained to accept the teachings of the faith and the authority of God's clergy without question. Unlike anyone else in my peer group, I embraced the penitential fasting of the holy seasons of Advent and Lent and liked how the physical depravations made my body feel. It gave me a sense of control at a time when I was constantly being seduced into surrender. My soul might belong to God but at least I still had some say over what happened to my body. I believed in the power of the Holy Sacraments and continued to share my deepest personal secrets with the priest in the confession box every Friday so I could be free from sin and ready to consume the physical body and blood of Jesus every Sunday. I believed in all of it fully and completely, forever and ever. Amen.

❧

AFTER THE STING of Montreal began to fade, the priest tempted me with another holy road trip. He invited me to join him on a pilgrimage to Rome over the upcoming summer holidays. He promised me that if I came, he would introduce me to the pope (then John Paul II). I was very excited at the possibility of seeing Europe on my first-ever vacation without my parents. Mom and Dad saw the trip as a learning opportunity and agreed to pay for the flight, provided I get a job and earn my own spending cash. I started mowing lawns and painting fences, and two months later I was boarding an overnight plane for Britain.

With its millions of people of every race, colour, and creed, London was a complete culture shock for a small boat boy from around the bay. So much to see and smell and taste and feel. A new world culture around every corner. My eyes and ears were popping right out of my adolescent head.

The priest bought me my first pint in a small pub outside Covent Garden. The warm beer initially tasted bitter but went down smoother as the alcohol helped me relax. After three pints, I remember feeling warm and fuzzy as we slowly navigated the noisy London crowds back to our hotel.

After lingering a few days and learning how to really enjoy a pint, I made my way with the priest down to Paris via ferry from Dover. I remember keenly feeling the absence of the English language as we checked into our tiny two-bunk hotel room on Île Saint-Louis. We spent our first day visiting religious shrines such as the Notre Dame Cathedral and kneeling in prayer at the rue du Bac chapel before the dead, but purportedly unde-composed, body of Saint Catherine Labouré. I remember looking dubitably at the ancient wax-covered corpse of the "incorruptible" saint and thinking she looked more like a mannequin than a French maid. I wondered if she felt claustrophobic in her tiny glass prison, always watched by eyes wanting something from her. This was my first time in a foreign country—not to mention my first time being so far away from my parents—and I was beginning to feel a little bit lost and lonely, so I bought her "miraculous" medal and put it around my sixteen-year-old neck for divine protection. The initial buzz of big-boy bravado was quickly fading and I missed my mom.

That night the priest introduced me to another strong and powerful spirit: Courvoisier Napoleon Cognac. I still remember the rush to the head this burning hard liquor brought on. My face was hot and my young heart felt like it was about to explode. After several shots I remember walking across the street and buying a pack of Gitanes. I had never smoked before and the strong French tobacco made me feel dizzy and weak. I downed another cognac and the City of Lights began to spin around me. I have only flashes of what happened next.

I remember being helped out of my chair and trying to march down the street singing "La Marseillaise."

I remember the priest putting on his Inspector Clouseau accent and trying to initiate mock combat, with me as Cato.

I remember trying to play along with his game.

I remember falling down and having to be helped back up.

I remember being sick over a bridge.

I remember wrestling in our hotel room.

I remember being overpowered and having my face pushed into a pillow and not being able to breathe.

I remember my jeans being pulled down.

The sting of a belt.

And then pain.

I had always been able to hold my own physically against the priest but I was loaded drunk and easily overpowered.

Helpless.

CUT...

♡

I'VE BEEN TOLD my early childhood was good. I honestly don't remember much of it. I've heard from my mom on multiple occasions how "challenging" I was because I kept "testing" her authority (her story). And I've heard I was "happy" and had a "pretty whimsical childhood" (Dad's story). Not sure who I believe, or if I believe it at all, as both parents have shown themselves to be very gifted creators of their own realities. Experiencing and living with that disconnect has been my reality since I was about twelve years old.

My mom told me one night while we were partying together (yes, I partied with my mom) that my older sister and I were conceived to save my parents' marriage. The fact that they divorced when I was in eighth grade should perhaps make me feel like something of a failure, but my parents were horrible together and getting a divorce was definitely the best way forward for the both of them.

From the age of twelve my sister, Jamie (two years older), and I very clearly became a source of competition for my mother in the quest for my father's love. Of course father-daughter love is very different than romantic love, but by this time in her marriage my mom was desperate for any kind of love. Basically, Mom resented whatever affection Dad showed me and my sister. Mom didn't need to say anything for us to understand the implicit competition we were engaged in; she just kind of stopped being a mom. I no longer had a mother but rather a "friend" in the woman whose home I shared. Mom's maternal instincts had moved out along with Dad and the three of us were left vying for scraps of affection and attention. Emotionally we were on our own, left to learn from the nuns in our Catholic school about our bodies, sex (or abstinence from it), and what being a good girl meant. On the other hand, my father had his own parenting problems, in that parenting got in the way of his many extramarital affairs.

Love and loyalty were elusive in our family.

While all this was going on, Jamie had already started to understand her new role in our evolving family dynamic. She very quickly went from self-involved teenager to involuntary pseudo-parent. Though we never spoke about it as children, it was completely understood that I would, for the most part, listen to her and follow her lead when it came to maneuvering within our family. She was the most stable of us all, so I gravitated to her. She was beautiful, strong and fierce in her defense against Dad's phantom demons and Mom's spineless mothering efforts. I was in awe of her. If it's ever taken a toll on her, I have no idea. To this day Jamie stands mostly silent and stoic, but there is no doubt she was determined not to follow in our parents' paths with her own family, and with me.

I believe my mom must have told herself a number of stories to get by during that time. More than once, a girlfriend of Dad's would call the house. The most brazen would actually ask for my dad, and when pressed "Who can I say is calling?" either hung up or mused, "A friend." Then there was the girl who parked her car outside our house to pick Dad up for their vacation—what he had called a "work trip." Yet, through it all, I watched my mom stick with him and lap up whatever little crumbs of affection he threw her way. Unfortunately, the majority of my memories of my mom are of her in her bedroom smoking, drinking Pepsi, and sleeping.

As a preteen girl, it was slowly but surely seeping into my head that being young and pretty were traits to be admired and would afford me love and attention. I was also learning that ignoring an issue, no matter how huge, was an easier and less painful way to deal with it than facing it head-on. "Philanderer" and "Doormat" were my two preteen role models, and I would embody both of these clichés later on in my own life.

It's only now, thirty years later, that I understand the ramifications of growing up with emotionally unavailable parents. But the twelve-year-old me just wanted Mom and Dad to notice her, to love her, to parent her.

Without that support from them, my sister became my surrogate parent. She was only two years older, which didn't leave much room for experience, but she stepped into the role as best she could and stays firmly planted there today.

I was hurt. I was angry. I was sad. Why weren't we enough for my dad? Why did Mom not even want to talk to me? Forget about them not having a relationship; I didn't care that they were barely together. I didn't care about their marriage. I was completely selfish and simply wanted my parents to be my mom and dad.

I managed to keep all the emotional wolves at bay by staying busy with competitive gymnastics, but when that ended so too did my ability to ignore my feelings of pain, hurt, and worthlessness. Around the time I turned fifteen, the wheels came off completely and my tenuous emotional stability dissolved.

It was around this time that I began to control my feelings with food. Eating as much as I could and then making myself throw up was a form of absolute control in a situation where I had none. Soon, eating as little as possible to see how much I could stand garnered me even greater control. Taking diet pills to the point of passing out on a shower floor seemed like not only a very grown-up, controlled decision but also one that had to elicit a response (attention) from my parents. I was taken to the hospital to have my stomach pumped. Even my dad had to interrupt his "work" trip to come see me in the hospital. Surely I would register some consideration and love now.

Nope.

So I started cutting.

I didn't know what cutting was. I didn't even know it was a "thing." All I remember is that I found a straight-edge razor, the kind used in box cutters, and wondered how it would feel to cut myself, just a little, on the inside of my wrist. I tried it, just enough to scratch my skin. *Wimp,* I remember thinking. *Try harder.* So I did. And a teeny tiny line appeared. I was pleased with myself. I told myself to do something, and I did it. I wasn't a wimp. I wasn't a failure. *Try again. Harder. See what happens. Not too hard, though, you don't want to hit a vein!* So I just kept going.

Little by little I etched away the skin with the straight-edge until I saw blood coming, just barely, out of the wound. It hurt, but not enough to make me stop, and I remember revelling in the sting. It was nice to finally feel some physical pain to match the emotional pain I'd been feeling for so very long. It was control and release all at once. Yes it hurt, but I also got a sort of high from it. The endorphins allowed me to push through any uncomfortable edginess and continue with the other wrist until I had two matching crimson cuts.

Angel wings.

I sat there and stared at those wounds slowly bleeding and felt very, very pleased with myself.

THE ROAD
TO ROME

THE NEXT MORNING I remember waking up naked in bed with my best friend, my confessor, my priest. It was still dark. I didn't know what to do, so I slowly grabbed my clothes and slunk into the tiny washroom and sat on the toilet, waiting for the sun to rise and trying not to vomit. When the priest woke up, he tried to make a joke about me being an "alcoholic" and then proceeded to pretend that nothing had happened. He just pulled on his civilian clothes and went out to find us some coffee and croissants for breakfast. I'm not sure if it was the physical after-effects of my first hangover or the mental trauma of the attack, but I was far too sick to eat breakfast while the priest plotted our course for the day, spilling butter and jam on a large fold-out map stretched across the very bed he'd just sexually assaulted me in. Business as usual. Nothing new here.

As we drove away from the city, I prayed to forget everything I had learned in Paris.

The next few days were relatively quiet as we slowly made our way over the Alps and down into Italy, but our liquor consumption began to increase as we got closer to Rome. I tried to monitor my drinking in an effort to avoid finding myself in any further compromising positions like the one in Paris, which still remained unmentioned. The priest, however, showed no signs of holding back, and I spent several nights fighting off his drunken physical advances. While walking back to our hotel in Venice one night he asked me for a hug, but I refused because I knew he wanted more. He slapped me hard across the face and then began to weep.

"I'm so sorry, Séan. Please don't tell your father. I'm just so lonely and you are my only friend in this world. All I want is a hug, I promise. Please let me hold you, Séan...please...."

I was just sixteen years old in a foreign country with my priest sobbing like a baby and his pants slowly slipping to his knees. He tried to kiss me but he missed my mouth and ended up licking my neck. I could hear him screaming my name as I ran off into the darkness.

I spent the night walking the streets alone because I had no money and nowhere else to go. This was back in 1983, long before the internet, and cellphones the size of milk cartons were extremely expensive and rare. My only other option would be to turn myself in to the Italian police, and the thought of that terrified me even more than returning to the priest. What I really wanted was to be back home with my family, with everything back the way it used to be, like none of this ever happened. I found my way back to the hotel and sat in the hallway in front of our shared room and waited until I heard stirring from within. A few minutes later he emerged. He looked very frightened and dishevelled. He was instantly apologetic when he saw me curled up on the floor and promised it would never happen again. We both agreed to forget the "foolishness" of the night before and mention it no more.

When we finally arrived in Rome, we secured cheap lodging at a monastery full of hairy old monks and went about seeking some clerical connections. The priest was determined to impress me by fulfilling his promise of getting me close to the pope. I don't know how he managed it, but on our second night in the city I got to receive the pontiff's personal blessing.

We were brought to the Vatican by an old Italian priest and hustled silently through several long, dark marble corridors whose walls were covered with priceless and ancient art. I saw no evidence of any vows of poverty or personal sacrifice as we enjoyed our VIP ALL ACCESS backstage pass. This internationally recognized corporate city-state reeked of obscene wealth and sweet incense. Eventually, we entered a large room with plush red carpets and painted gold walls. To my surprise, the room was full of teenaged boys: young seminarian wannabes with their clerical mentors and chaperones just like me. I wondered who else was sorry they had come. As I took a knee and kissed the pontiff's ring I heard him whisper softly in my ear, "Peace on you."

LOSING MY RELIGION

I LEFT NEWFOUNDLAND an innocent kid. A virgin. I came back with the burden of a dark secret that would haunt my entire life, and a thirst for liquor that would help drown it out.

I decided I would never tell anyone. I was angry and ashamed and I blamed myself for what had happened. I decided to keep my secret buried in alcohol and live alone with my guilt and self-loathing, and that's a lot to take on when you've just turned sixteen. Even if I told the truth, no one would believe me, so I felt that pretending nothing had happened was the easiest way forward. The priest was also a good pretender; he went right back to being our daily unannounced house guest. Dad continued to loan him money and Mom kept cooking him his favourite meals. We were all one big happy fucked-up holy family.

This facade went on for the next two years of high school. I continued to go to mass and say the rosary and I continued to confess my sins to my "best friend" on a weekly basis. I also began to drink more. This could be seen as a normal progression for most Newfoundland teenagers, but my consumption was always fuelled by a deeper desire to forget. I drank as often as I could to help numb the pain I was forced to face daily as my abuser walked freely in my own home. I may have been singing in the choir but by grade eleven I was definitely no altar boy.

The priest had stolen my virginity and shaken my faith. My former piety was now gone and my interest in the church and all things holy much diminished. My parents began to accept the fact that the priesthood would likely not be my vocation after all. Unfettered now by my former religious convictions, I allowed myself to fall in love again with pretty teenaged girls. I just wanted to feel normal in spite of what had happened to me, and making out in the back seat of my dad's American Concord was an excellent way to forget.

Undeterred and likely delusional, the priest frequently tried to inter-fere in my dating life by going behind my back and warning my mom about certain parish "bad girls" I'd do best to avoid. He even tried to set me up with a devout few he knew would never "put out," but I was having none of it. I had seen all I needed at this point to know that a priest was something I would never be.

The priest was still at our house almost every day but I had my driver's license now, which made me harder for him to hunt. If his car was parked in front of our house as I approached, I would just keep driving around until it was gone. If my mom told me the priest had called and would be coming over for dinner, I would try to find some excuse not to show up. My parents simply wrote my aloofness off as ordinary teenage angst.

The more I pulled away, the more guilty pressure the priest continued to apply. He would leave long, elaborate letters in my bedroom quoting scripture and questioning my faith, trying to guilt me into spending more time with him alone. The more he pushed, the more I drank.

I somehow managed to keep my marks up and graduated from high school in 1985 and moved on to higher education at Memorial University Newfoundland (MUN). After my obligatory first semester in general studies, I realized the path of least resistance to alcohol-induced bliss lay not through math (a made-up language I have always struggled with) or science, but via the arts. I littered my course load with literature and philosophy and quickly found myself in very articulate, frothy, and fun-loving company. It didn't take long to focus my "efforts" on theatre, a land of make-believe, where the players were all fluent in pretending, and partying was seen more like a religion than a lifestyle. The next four years of my academic life would be devoted to drinking and fucking and forgetting.

❧

GEORGE STREET IS less than three hundred yards away from the Atlantic Ocean but unlike the rest of my fair home province, it isn't postcard pretty. Dirty and often dangerous, this mecca for dedicated boozers soaks up far more than its fair share of national rum sales. George Street is where Canadians go to get DRUNK.

On my nineteenth birthday I began working as a busboy at Greensleeves, one of George Street's sleaziest pickup bars. Blue-eyed and barely legal, I quickly became popular with the much older and predominantly female crowd. Most of the regulars were in their early forties and already working on their second or third marriages and I was quickly labelled "cougar bait" by the rest of the staff. I got a lot of tips and free drinks in exchange for my tight young ass being made available for groping and sometimes more. On more than one occasion, I was dragged body and bones into the female washrooms and held hostage by horny divorcees until I gave them what they wanted: a ride home. The facilities were furnished with condom dispensers and I remember having to ask one of my first dates how to use one. Birth control was still a sin where I came from. Up until now, pulling out early and praying hard after were the only prophylactics I knew.

This new late-night lifestyle didn't sit well with my folks, so it wasn't long before I moved out and shacked up with one of my patrons. My parents were disappointed of course, but they seemed to take it in stride (wild oats and the sowing of them, etc.).

The priest lost his mind.

I wouldn't see him, and he couldn't come to my place of work without destroying his reputation, so he began to write me long and rambling letters almost immediately after I took the busboy job. They would often start off polite, invoking the scriptures or the famous last words of some ancient saint. Then they would get personal, telling me how much he missed our friendship and asking why I had abandoned my faith...and him. They always ended with guilt and rage. I remember wondering what my parents might think of these epistles. Would they see the sick man on the other side of the page? Or would they continue to be deceived by the devil I had come to know? I wasn't really sure how they would react to the truth. I was convinced that coming clean would end in pain for someone either way. And most likely that would be me. Any attempt at revelation would ultimately require a full disclosure of what happened in Europe, and none of us were ready for that. So I hid the letters between the pages of my old birthday gift, Father Alban Butler's extensive anthology of the holy "who's who." There they would sit, hidden in plain view on the bookshelf of my old bedroom back home. My soul might be going to hell but its secrets would be safe with the saints.

The bar became my haven; the one place I could always be free of the priest's malignant presence. My life there was liquid and loose and I began to like it very much—until one night the manager passed me the phone.

"It's for you. Says it's urgent. Sounds pretty drunk. Crazy fucker says he's a priest...."

I pulled the cord as far away from the noisy crowd as I could and knelt down on the floor behind the bar to keep out of sight. I could hear the priest crying even before I got the phone up to my ear. He was loaded drunk and all over the place.

"How can you do this to me? How can you do this to God?

"I love you and God loves you but you will have to pay for your sins. Stop this and come back to me now, Séan. Come back to God before it's too late."

"This is where I work. Please never call me here again."

"You are a filthy little WHORE—"

I hung up the phone and ordered the first of what would become way too many double Dark 'n' Dirtys (black rum and Coke). By the time my shift was over I was completely fucked up and still fuming. I headed out into the night looking for a fight. George Street is renowned for its amateur pugilists so it didn't take me very long to find one. A few dirty looks and the next thing I know I'm rolling around on the sidewalk in a flurry of punches and kicks, screaming bloody murder. I'm not much good with my fists so the brawl didn't last very long. I remember being scraped off the street and tossed roughly into a Royal Newfoundland Constabulary paddy wagon, scratched to pieces and covered in blood. They hauled me off to the lockup where they took my shoelaces and my belt. Then they threw me into a piss-reeking cement cell full of belligerent booze-bags. And there I lay, on the cold hard floor, until I sobered up the next morning.

So much for sanctuary.

Shortly after my brief incarceration, the priest was reassigned to a small rural parish in Placentia Bay. I'm not sure why. Maybe the Church needed to cover up the sexual indiscretions of the priest in that parish? After all, moving pedophiles around has long proven to be a successful tactic in the Catholic church. Placentia was a four-hour drive from St. John's so the priest's visits to our house became much less frequent, which, for me, was a welcomed relief. For the rest of the family, especially my parents, his presence was very much missed. They couldn't understand why I wouldn't make more time for my old friend who was now living in exile around the bay.

The priest kept begging me to come visit him until I reluctantly agreed, only to please my parents. The plan was for me and another mutual friend to drive out and spend the night at the priest's new place. When he picked me up on Saturday morning, my heart sank: the other passenger (if there had ever really been one) had called in sick. I would be flying solo again with my old abuser.

We headed out on the highway with Beethoven's Symphony no. 3 on full blast. The priest was in very high spirits.

The drinking started immediately with the purchase of a case of beer as we fuelled up just outside the overpass, so we were already buzzed when we arrived at the priest's new home later that afternoon. I was wary and uncomfortable but by now I really liked to drink, and my inner alcoholic couldn't resist taking full advantage of his well-stocked bar while I waited for what I knew would eventually come.

As the night wore on and the gin took effect, the priest's mood began to swing violently. He told me how much he missed me and then berated me for being a lapsed Catholic and a bad friend. He warned me that although Jesus loved me, if I continued to ignore his vocational call I would be forever damned. After all that had transpired up to this point, he still believed that the priesthood was my true calling. With Beethoven still blaring and my head beginning to spin, I decided to take my leave while I could still walk and quietly made my way downstairs to the guestroom in the basement, where I proceeded to pass out.

There was no lock on the door.

I came to some time later when I felt the priest behind me, grinding himself up against my ass. He was wearing nothing but his underwear and I could feel his hairy chest heaving deeply and smell his foul, liquored breath.

I thought about getting up and running for the car keys.

I thought about beating him to death and burning his house down.

I thought about the Virgin Mary and wondered if she was watching.

I thought about killing myself by jumping off a cliff.

But in the end I did nothing.

I pretended to be asleep and I let the assault continue until I felt his disgusting warm wet cover my lower back. When he was finished, he got off me and staggered back up to his bedroom.

The next morning nothing was said. We drank some tea and he offered to hear my confession because he wanted to make sure I was in a "state of grace" and able to receive communion, but I declined. We walked across the street where he celebrated mass. The congregation was small and old and I was very noticeably the only one who did not go up to the altar to receive my Saviour, which led to some sideways glances that greatly embarrassed the priest. My own minor religious rebellion. After the service, he began to lecture me on the importance of the Sacrament of Reconciliation and asked why I had chosen not to avail myself of his divine services prior to the mass. I took his car keys off the table and told him I wanted to go home and that I would tell my parents everything if we didn't leave right now.

We drove back to St. John's in silence. He dropped me off in the drive-way and as he drove away I resolved to never see the man again.

To this day I feel sick whenever I hear Beethoven.

...AND PASTE

I KEPT CUTTING through my sophomore and most of my junior year of high school. It stopped after I'd had a particularly vigorous cutting session and ended up calling my friend Julie and telling her I wasn't sure what I was going to do, that she needed to come over as soon as possible. I was sixteen, sitting on my bathroom counter, door wide open, no one home, music as loud as my little boom box would go. I had the water in the sink running and I wanted to see how deep I could cut before the pain was too much. I had thought about what dying would be like. I had thought about committing suicide. It seemed both an easy solution and a permanent one. But it was for both of those reasons that I eventually ruled it out as an option. I in no way deserved *easy* and the idea of anything being *permanent* at that age was abhorrent to me. I had thought about what I would do if I actually hit my vein, but none of that danger superseded my need to feel the pain. I hated feeling so lonely, so desperate, and unable to do anything about my home life. At least with cutting, I was in control.

Julie came running into the house and saw the blood running freely from both my wrists as I held them under water. I remember seeing panic in her eyes. I remember seeing hurt in her eyes. And maybe disappointment, too. But at the same time, I saw her *seeing* me and I knew that I mattered, at least to her, and that was enough for me to stop cutting. I was done with it.

But I still needed to hold on to that feeling of control, and voluntarily throwing up afforded me this, absolutely. I would continue with the bulimia until and throughout my first marriage. In this one very small area of my life, I was queen. I ruled that kingdom of silent suffering with swiftness, efficiency, and secrecy for the better part of ten years.

It is still a daily battle not to throw up. Everyone needs food to live; I couldn't and can't exorcise it from my life. It is the devil I'll have to live with forever.

❦

I WENT TO a Jesuit college in the Midwest after high school to study anything but business. I knew that whatever I did, I did not want to end up in the family business with my dad and sister. So I majored in political science…and ended up working for the family business with my dad and my sister. I chose this particular university not because it was where I really wanted to go, but because they told me I would only be accepted on a probationary basis. Basically, when I heard they didn't want me, I set out to prove to the institution that I could hack it. And I did. But it wasn't pretty. I even finagled my way into a congressional internship in Washington, DC, for the summer between my sophomore and junior years, without the grades or the recommendations required (thank God for sorority sisters' connections!), and that's where I met my first husband. Who knew that long-distance relationships and dramatic romances would be my forte?

Tony was seven years older than me, and his twenty-six to my nineteen was a chasm that proved too deep to overcome. He was an engineer with a sweet southern accent and a crewcut that made me think he was military when I met him in a bar that summer. We went out a few times and started to become what I thought was serious when suddenly he broke up with me. I wasn't having it, and I convinced him that the distance and age difference weren't insurmountable. I was just twenty-two when we got married, one of the first in my high-school graduating class to do so. I was also probably one of the first to get a divorce, four and a half years later.

Husband #1 had a temper and I had faithfulness issues (thanks, Dad). Being monogamous didn't seem that important to me. I had been shown how to treat relationships by my father and I'd taken his lessons to heart. My husband and I weren't even married before I started down the crooked path of cheating. This continued throughout our short, tumultuous marriage, as did our inability to effectively communicate…ever.

Not being mature enough for marriage hadn't stopped me from getting married. I remember it seeming like an escape from my all-encompassing family, who, up until that point, knew every aspect of my life. It was as much "control" as I could wield. I was working for the family business, which at that time was a consulting firm for minority business owners. In the beginning, Husband #1 and I were living in Minnesota. The day after my sister got married, we moved to North Carolina. Four years later, we moved back to Minnesota, and six months after that we were divorced. I was back to working for the family business. I guess the false sense of security it offered was too strong to ignore.

A couple of years later, everything started going downhill with our business. I found myself on the hook financially and emotionally to a company I had no ownership or control over. I had remortgaged my condo to help pay the company payroll for a few months. I had also maxed out my credit cards paying for product for the business. And that's to say nothing of all of the time, effort, and heart I put into this failing organization.

I started drinking.

I was going out at least four or five nights a week and coming home very drunk most of the time. I thought I had it all handled; as long as my day-life wasn't affected by my nightlife, all was good. But there was that one time I had to be rushed to the hospital when I was at work because I was doubled over with an excruciating pain in my stomach. Turned out I had polyps in my colon. Turned out those can definitely be caused by alcohol abuse. There was also that one time—or six—I had to call in sick to work because I was too hungover to make it in. And there may have been too many times to count when I was late to the job because of my drinking. So maybe I didn't have it handled. And unfortunately, working in a family business doesn't afford one any privacy. But to be honest, I didn't have to reel it in very much because I had the perfect drinking buddy in my dad.

I always thought Dad had just been a social drinker, but as I reflected on earlier memories, I began to realize that he had always been quite the drinker himself. "Functioning alcoholic" (sometimes not-so-functioning) is probably more like it. It seems to me he was trying to suppress a lot of the horrible memories he had (and still has) about his time in Vietnam, and when he was drunk he could either completely forget or simply not worry about what he said. Either way he was going to squash those demons with booze. I had no way of knowing this same situation would rear its ugly head in my own marriage, years later.

The big joke between my sister and me is about all the holidays we hate. Christmas meant Dad stayed back at the house while we went to midnight Mass with Mom and by the time we got home he was pretty drunk...then either the fighting ensued or just the nasty comments. Merry Christmas. Fourth of July was pretty much just constant beer-drinking all day; most weekends were the same. My thirtieth birthday was an embarrassment of Dad getting drunk at the restaurant where we were celebrating and him berating me in front of my sister, her husband, and my boyfriend at the time. Nice dinners out were always capped off with concern about whether or not Dad would "cross the Rubicon" (his metaphor, not ours). My father fancying himself Julius Caesar should have given me a clue about the animal inside him.

Because my dad was the sole owner of the business, his drinking and temper became more frequent and unpredictable as the company became more and more insolvent. I'd always given him a pass on his drinking, especially when I was the one getting drunk with him. Even when he veered into the asshole category when drunk, I overlooked it, because if he wasn't okay then I probably wasn't either. I usually knew when we were in asshole territory because he would say, "But have you ever killed anyone, Andrea? Answer me that...have you?" I'd know then that we were in for a ride. As a Vietnam vet, he never spoke about his time "in country," and thunderclouds appeared in his eyes if it was ever brought up. Clearly, he had issues. My sister and I never even gave it a second thought that he had PTSD; of course he did, any casual observer could see that. It's tragic to me that he himself didn't come to that conclusion until he was seventy-two years old.

At this point, about five years after I started working for my father, the family business had morphed into the manufacturing and installation of energy management systems. Despite its attempt at evolution, however, the company was crumbling—and this was in no small part due to my dad's ego. Yes, the economy played a part in its demise, but my father's inability to face the truth—his spending habits, his poor business decisions, and his unwillingness to listen to his daughters (whom he had always told he trusted the most) but instead listen to other men who may not have had his best interests at heart—helped speed up and solidify the eventual bankruptcy of the business he had built over three decades.

I'd finally had enough of my father's excuses for not opening tax bills and continuing to spend money like we had it. I'd grown fed up with being a scapegoat even though I had no decision-making power. And my soul had grown weary of seeing someone I once admired drown in his own ego and destructiveness. So I did the only thing a truly brave person would do...I turned tail and ran to the mountains.

As if a toxic family business wasn't excuse enough to leave, I was three years post-divorce and still meandering from one pointless or pernicious relationship to another. If I was seeing someone, I was never faithful, and I thought nothing of bringing home a different man every so often to keep my bed warm. The two serious relationships I had post-divorce were riddled with cheating (me); I gave just enough of myself to keep these guys on the hook for as long as I needed them to make me feel whole. They were both sweet guys who deserved far more than I was ever going to give them, but the selfish me just continued using them to get what I needed. I was drinking almost every night, most nights coming to just the soberish side of completely loaded, driving the two miles to and from my neighborhood bar with one eye closed to keep the road straight. I was miserable. I was hurt and so far from confident in who I was I didn't want to be me anymore. You know the feeling when you wake up and you just wish you were someone else? Drinking helped me forget how useless I was; but then in the morning when I could barely function, I felt even more worthless than the day before. It was a cycle that I kept repeating, my own self-fulfilling prophecy. I had come so far from my high-school and college years of eating disorders and cutting only to see myself right back there ten years later.

I was desperate to break away from the person I saw myself becoming, the person resembling my dad. More likely, though, the person I was trying to get away from the most was me. How do you outrun yourself? Booze wasn't working anymore; it was just making me sick and causing more stress. My sister was busy not only with the chaos of the company, but also with her young and growing family of three small children, and therefore could not hand-hold me like she had in the past. That's when I decided I had to do the most drastic thing I could think of—move away, by myself, to a place where I had no job, no friends, and no idea what it could offer me.

WHY GO TO HELL?

A BOUT A MONTH after I vowed never to see the priest again, in early January 1988, my parents called to tell me he had been in an "accident." He was in the hospital recovering and was asking to see me. I told them I would visit when I got a chance but Mom pushed for us all to go in as a family to show our support. I didn't want to go but wasn't quick enough to come up with a good excuse, and before I could put down the phone they were already on their way to pick me up.

As we approached St. Clare's Mercy Hospital, a wave of nausea washed over me. I began to hear Beethoven in my head as Dad explained that the priest had actually suffered some kind of "mental breakdown" and was being treated for exhaustion and depression. Apparently there had been some kind of "incident" with the RCMP but nobody was hurt and "everything was going to be okay."

By "incident," my mom meant that the priest had picked up a young male hitchhiker while driving around with an open bottle of booze. A few hours and several bottles later, he'd pulled over in front of a Pentecostal temple, grabbed his .22 out of the trunk, and fired two rounds straight through the "enemy's" front window.

Here are some excerpts from legal transcripts of the case:

> At about 9:57 P.M. the accused who with a companion had been drinking alcoholic beverages off and on during the day, stopped his vehicle opposite the Miracle Tabernacle on the TransCanada Highway, took a .22 caliber rifle from the back of his vehicle and discharged two shots into the upper panel of the windows facing the road. It appears that he was aiming his shot at a sign within the building exhibiting the slogan:

"Why Go to Hell". He then got back in his motor vehicle and drove towards Gander, a distance of approximately 25 miles. He was apprehended by the Royal Canadian Mounted Police enroute approximately ten minutes later and taken into custody, where he remained until the next morning. The pastor was in the building at the time the shots were fired and had just left the room containing the window which had been punctured by the bullets discharged by the accused when the incident occurred.

The priest got off easy and was charged only with the unlawful discharge of a firearm. This alone should have been very big news, but the incident was hushed up by the RCMP and ignored by the press. Here's what the priest had to say in his own defence:

He declared that he had been suffering from insomnia for two and a half weeks immediately before this incident, during which period he could not sleep for more than two hours in any day. He declared that he does not have an alcohol problem and that his normal drinking habits are conservative. He offered no explanation for his conduct on the occasion in question except to say that he was concerned at that time that he would not be able to sleep that night and with bedtime approaching he was under considerable tension because of it. He stated that he "just cracked" (to use his own expression) and when he saw the sign in the temple, it came into his head to smash it and so he fired at it forthwith. The accused has expressed great remorse over his conduct which he alleges is completely out of character with his normal behaviour.

Here's what he had to say about the illegal weapon:

He stated that it had been his habit to carry a .22 caliber rifle in the back of his motor vehicle while travelling on the highway. On such occasions he would stop at some point along the way, boil the kettle and engage in target practice using tin cans as targets.

And here's what his high-profile Catholic doctor had to say on his behalf:

> Doctor X [name redacted by author], a general medical practitioner and for many years a friend of the accused, testified on his behalf. He knew the accused as a member of his parish, as a patient, and as a friend. He said the accused was a dedicated priest, much beloved by his parishoners. Doctor X declared he found the accused to be an extremely committed clergyman dedicated to his work and his priesthood which was the paramount object in his life. He was aware that the accused would take an occasional drink of alcohol, but had never seen him take more than that. He found that the accused was an intense, caring and dedicated person who perhaps worked too hard.

The case didn't even make it to trial. In the end, the priest got off with only probation and was asked to provide the Pentecostal pastor (who could very well have been killed) financial restitution for the windows he had damaged. He was also ordered not to possess a firearm for five years.

One might think this bizarre and highly illegal episode would expose the cleric as the very dangerous offender he really was, but no. Instead of ire and indignation, all he drew from his faithful followers, my parents included, was pity and concern. When we walked into his private room filled with get-well cards and bouquets of fresh-cut flowers, the priest had a huge smile on his face. I remember silently standing at the foot of his bed staring at his feet while Dad made small talk and Mom fussed over him. While he lay there soaking up their attention, I heard him call my name.

"Séan...come closer and give the poor priest a hug."

I could feel my face turning red as I looked up slowly to face my abuser. His arms were open, waiting for my embrace, and my parents' eyes were on me, waiting for me to offer it. Time stopped, and for a split second I felt like the truth would come falling out of me like rain. But I still wasn't ready for the truth and all that fell were tears. Without saying a word, I turned around and walked out of the hospital and back home. My parents assumed that I had been emotionally overwhelmed by my deep sympathy for my stricken friend and I lacked the courage to correct them. My tears that day were from blinding frustration and innocence taken.

My tears that day were for myself.

After getting out of the hospital and off with everything else, the priest was quietly shuffled away to England for further "treatment" and a fresh start.

I would like to point out that through all this I continued to cling to what little remained of my faith. I went to mass with my family on the holiest holidays and even the occasional Sunday, when I wasn't too hungover to drag my ass out of bed. To that end, I even secured a new confessor who just happened to be the resident exorcist (according to the rules, every parish was supposed to have one). Monsignor Morrissey was as ancient as he was old-school. A surly, red-faced giant of a man, he had little mercy and even less patience for the demonic. As a fully and completely indoctrinated Catholic, my approach to the Sacrament of Reconciliation was to hold absolutely nothing back. I was living a life of sin and breaking all the rules, but the confessional provided me with a relatively easy way to repeatedly make things right. It was a divinely inspired Get Out of Jail Free card. I could sin all I wanted but still get to heaven as long as I made it into the confessional at least once a week. Ingenious. The old monsignor was initially impressed by my complete candor, but after hearing me repeat the same mortal sins over and over again every Friday for three months, he got wise to my wicked way of thinking.

"Are you truly sorry for your sins, my son?"

"Yes, Father."

"And are you honestly trying to avoid the near occasions of sin?"

"...Father?"

"Are you actually trying to change your ways and do better?"

"No, Father."

"Then why do you continue to seek absolution from me?"

"So I can get into heaven when I die, Father."

"Then you are abusing the sacrament and I can no longer absolve you."

If this were a blackjack table in Vegas, I would have just been made for counting the cards.

I haven't been back to confession or mass since.

I did have one more very improbable run-in with the priest, several years after I walked out of his hospital room in tears. Great Big Sea was embarking on its first European tour and my bandmates and I were gathering our eclectic collection of baggage after clearing customs in London's Heathrow Airport. It was early in the morning and we were all feeling pretty tender after the overnight flight. A local friend at the airport in St. John's had bumped us up to first class, so the whiskey had been flowing freely for most of the evening.

As I sorted through the instruments to make sure none had been damaged, a feeling came over me like I was being watched. When I stood up and looked across the conveyor, I saw a familiar shadow on the other side of the belt. It was the old-fashioned clerical cassock I once wore so proudly as a Halloween costume. Above its pinched white collar was the ashen face of my former tormentor. For several seemingly endless seconds, we remained frozen in a dead-eyed stare. I had spent the past decade burying the truth in alcohol and drugs but now, as I stood face to face with my very own demon, all the pain of my past came boiling back.

He picked up his suitcase and walked towards me slowly.

"It's a small world after all. How are you doing, Séan?"

"I sing in a band now."

I broke out into a cold sweat.

"So I've heard. I hope you still make time for mass. How's your mom and dad doing?"

"Fine." Awkward silence. My stomach began to churn.

"I have to run along, but please give them my best and good luck with your band."

He walked away.

I walked into the lavatory and threw up.

Stone Cold Heart

There's a north wind blowing in the air tonight
I can feel it in the pale moonlight
There's a blackbird flying across the sky
Blood on his wing and fear in his eye
There's a mad dog barking at my back door
He's taking names and keeping score
Just like you
and your stone cold heart

There's a white flag hanging across the mast
The ghost of love that couldn't last
There's a fire burned out in a broken heart
over a bridge that's been ripped apart
There's a dark horse racing at a runaway train
He knows he ain't coming back again
Just like you
And your stone cold heart

Words unspoken, that look in your eyes
Our love is frozen in lies

There's a rib cage waiting for a rusty knife
A baby fighting for it's life
There's a blind man drowning across the bay
A black bat broken in an empty cave
There's a rumour out there running wild
She's dressed to kill and right in style
Just like you
and your stone cold heart

PART II

PSALMS

TAKE THIS ALL OF YOU
AND DRINK FROM IT

ST. JOHN'S IS the party capital of Canada.

With more bars per capita than any other city in North America and live music available in most of them, St. John's is our nation's own New Orleans. There are no social taboos against overconsumption and drinking to excess is an accepted and deliberate pastime. Whenever I went downtown from the ages of sixteen (which was technically illegal, but really not a problem) to forty-six (when I finally stopped), it was always with the sole intention of getting completely loaded—and I was not alone. There was always a phalanx of like-minded imbibers to have fun with when you entered the George Street "liquor zone." Before the oil boom of the early 2000s and the subsequent influx of cocaine and crime, St. John's was a much safer place to stumble the streets late at night completely bombed—a state I often found myself in.

I quickly became an expert in where to get the best deals on drinks and where all the good bands were playing. I've always been drawn to music, and singing in particular (I could sing "Paddy Murphy" at the age of two). Beyond that, my hometown spoiled me with an enviable surplus of excellent talent for seldom more than a five-dollar cover fee. I got to regularly see some amazing musical groups in intimate venues like Bridgett's Pub and The Ship Inn. I was never sober at these shows but the music always managed to cut through all the crap in my head and work its way into my badly damaged heart. Music connected and somehow always made me feel better even without a liquor buzz. It was with this in mind that, while studying for my Arts degree—and with no musical training whatsoever—I made the decision to become a professional singer.

St. John's is a city full of sleeveen show-offs and it didn't take me long to find some like-minded and willing onstage wannabes.

Bob Hallett sat behind me in Dr. Everard King's English Romantic Poetry class at MUN and in between Shelley and Keats we found ourselves discussing the lyrics of Joe Strummer and Shane MacGowan. Folk music had always been popular in Newfoundland but it was enjoying a resurgence worldwide in the late '80s and we wanted to be a part of this new, old, and exciting scene.

Our first band was called N.R.A. Not the "take this rifle from my cold dead hands" crowd but the "Newfoundland Republican Army." Because of our province's suspicious induction into Confederation, many of us Newfoundlanders (or at least townies) carried a considerable cultural chip around on our shoulders. Weary of remaining a "have-not" province, we dreamed of an independent, self-sufficient Newfoundland and felt that writing new songs of rebellion would be a sure recipe for revolutionary success. Take, for instance, N.R.A.'s only original composition, "The Republican Song":

> I was born on a St. John's street
> where all my hopes could meet defeat
> and the goal of all my friends was work in Canada
> but soon there'll come a day
> when the young will want to stay
> and learn again to rule their native land.

The band consisted of an unwieldy seven people and practiced for three months before our first show: a MUN talent contest, which we somehow managed to win. But the group quickly imploded under its own weight. After our second performance at The Grad House—a well-known unofficial fraternity house that hired bands for parties and sold booze without a license—we had a huge row and broke up due to political and sexual differences.

Undeterred by our first failed foray into the world of folk rock, Bob and I quickly picked up the pieces and formed a new band. "Rankin Street" was named for the address of the tiny basement apartment where we held our rehearsals. After some early shuffling of personnel, the band settled into a four-piece, including Jackie St. Croix on bass and Darrell Power on guitar.

I had first seen Darrell perform at the very small but highly influential Rose & Thistle Pub on Water Street. He had a large repertoire that encompassed everything from James Taylor to Pink Floyd. He never cut the ends of his guitar strings, preferring instead to let the wires flail about, often to the detriment of whoever shared his stage. He wore thick John Lennon glasses and had an easy and affable way with the audience. Recently he had gained some local notoriety by writing a parody song about our famous campus bar, "The Breezeway," a bluesy ode to student drinking, joint-smoking, and general time-wasting.

Darrell was human jukebox and I was impressed by the number of requests he was able to oblige the small but demanding audience. After his set I introduced myself and we stepped outside to smoke a joint of black hash, a ritual we would repeat at least a thousand times over the next fifteen years.

Rankin Street was not very good.

We could all sing, but the only member who could actually play his instrument well was Darrell. What we lacked in talent, however, we made up for in determination, and by carefully choosing a repertoire of popular Celtic cover songs, I was able to keep the little group gainfully employed four to five nights a week on the ever-expanding George Street circuit.

We got paid a hundred dollars each per show on average, which was just enough to pay the rent and buy enough hash to keep me well sedated. (Thirty years later, the same gig still pays a hundred dollars, which does not say much for the financial future of the modern-day "music industry.") For the most part, we drank for free and I partied through this haze for the better part of four years until I graduated with a degree in philosophy and dramatic arts and realized that my employment prospects were absolutely dreadful. Rankin Street had grown into a good pub band and had developed a loyal following, but I knew we had already gone as far as we were ever going to and decided to cut the cord and look for a real job.

Unfortunately, real jobs were very hard to find in Newfoundland back in the early '90s, especially jobs that allowed you to smoke hash all day and drink free booze all night, so I quickly found myself back in school pursuing a master's degree in folklore (like that would increase my employment potential). While the courses did keep me in contact with the music I loved, I found the academics of it all incredibly boring. I became restless, so I bought a guitar and taught myself how to play it. By the end of my first semester, I was bored right out of my mind and desperately wanted to start making music again. I knew that all these old books were never going to make me happy, so I began writing new songs. What I really needed now was a new band.

The early '90s was a time of great upheaval in Newfoundland. The northern cod fishery we all took for granted, and which had sustained us for five hundred years, was in free-fall, triggering a new wave of out-migration. The lucrative oil jobs we were all promised in high school were still a decade away from reality, and even the most well trained and highly educated were not immune to the severe employment drought. Once again, we watched our brightest and best leave for work and the promise of a better future.

> My father is gone now, and the fish are gone too
> Abused and mismanaged, oh what can we do?
> I'm too old to change, but what of my sons,
> How will they know that we weren't the ones?

> DFO regulations permitted the rape
> Of our beautiful ocean, from headland to cape
> They brought in big trawlers, they tore up our twine
> Politicians don't care for what's yours or what's mine!

> You brave Newfoundlanders, now listen to me
> Shove the package to hell and go back to the sea
> If we don't stand our ground, we will fade away
> And the bones of our fathers will turn in the clay

I spent my whole life out there on the sea
Some government bastard now takes it from me
It's not just the fish, they've taken my pride
I feel so ashamed that I just want to hide.

–From "Fisherman's Lament" written with my dad,
Ed McCann

Hard times have a long history of inspiring great music. The blues, country, reggae, and folk were all created to help soothe our pain and inspire our hearts on dark days, and Newfoundland music proved no exception to this healing tradition. The economy may have been in the toilet but the tunes kept rolling and the rum kept flowing. It really was a great scene to grow up in and I consider myself fortunate to have been a part of it.

After spending the better part of the previous four years slogging it out on a road to nowhere in the bars of St. John's, all of a sudden Toronto began to take a serious interest in our province's bright little music scene. The East Coast Music Awards, established in the 1980s to celebrate and recognize Atlantic artists, quickly became the best vehicle to showcase your work to the real music industry. Local songwriter and former Wonderful Grand Band front man Ron Hynes was the first to ink a deal, with EMI in 1992. He was followed soon after by local pub favourites The Irish Descendants, who were signed by Warner Music Canada. I began to feel a bit like I was missing the boat. I led myself to believe that real success might actually be achievable if I could just bring together the right combination of talents. With renewed hope, I decided to give the music thing one last try and set off again in search of collaborators.

Darrell was "in" even before I got to ask the question. Graduating with a degree in religious studies had left him as functionally unemployable as me and he now found himself languishing through an obligatory education degree. He, too, felt underwhelmed by the way Rankin Street had ultimately underachieved and was willing to give it one more chance. I could play a mean bodhrán (Irish goat-skinned hand drum) and carry a tune, but as much as I enjoyed making music I never actually craved the attention of the spotlight and preferred to focus more on songwriting and show promotion. I had a reputation for being one of the hardest "grinders" (a behind-the-scenes multitasking agent/manager/promoter/pest) in St. John's and my bands always made money. Rankin Street had become a tight little group by the end of its run but it lacked a charismatic leader to focus our audience's eyes. Determined to learn from my past mistakes, I set about seeking a shameless self-promoter who was willing to do just about anything to get people's attention.

Alan Doyle was performing in a duo called Staggering Home when I first laid eyes on him at the Rose & Thistle pub. The act was rough and very "blue" in the style of other comedic gross-out acts MacLean and MacLean and, more locally, Lambert and James. The schtick was mostly vulgar musical parody, which went over really well with the local pubsters. Their biggest "hit" was arguably a parody of the *Sesame Street* classic "In Your Neighbourhood," in which they tried to humorously subvert the educational children's song by populating it with dangerous neighbours like "child molesters" and "parish priests."

While this song did bring back some very disturbing personal memories, I was attracted to the fearless irreverence with which the new verses were delivered and by the incredible ball of raw energy from whence they came. There were fewer than a dozen people in the pub that night and half of those were Alan's family, but he played the room like it was Wembley Stadium. He even went so far as to set up his own spotlight so we could all see him that much better through the blue haze of tobacco smoke that filled the room. Alan Doyle demanded the audience's attention and was relentless in its pursuit. I knew straight away that he was the right man for the job.

Darrell, Alan, and I played our first and only show together as a trio under the unfortunate moniker and local slang term "Best Kind" (Newfoundland English for "all is well") at the Rose & Thistle in early spring of 1993. I don't remember a single thing about the gig other than it was jammed full (about fifty people). Since then I've had at least five hundred people tell me they were at that pivotal performance, and by all accounts we were absolutely fantastic. Our reputation as a new "St. John's supergroup" spread fast, and the following month we were invited to open for our recently signed friends, The Irish Descendants, at the MUN Gym (capacity one thousand). It was "a buck a beer" and our new band was going over really well with the extremely inebriated young crowd when Bob Hallett surprised us all by showing up at the gig and jumping onstage with his mandolin for the last two songs. He'd been away on the mainland looking for work but had flown home when he caught wind of what we were up to. As the crowd screamed for more, he told us he wanted "in" too, provided we agreed to abandon our "stupid fucking name."

Things started to happen really fast for us after that. We were all in our mid-twenties and had managed to learn a few hard lessons along the way. We really wanted things to work out this time so we decided to record immediately, while our energy was fresh. The plan was to target the 1994 ECMAs, which were being held in St. John's, in the hope of attracting some Toronto major-label attention. We were all very focused, and what we may have lacked in talent we more than made up for in dedication and enthusiasm. But we still needed a name. After much debate we settled on the title track, "Great Big Sea"—not because it was anyone's favourite, but because it offended the majority of shareholders the least. The song is about the tsunami that struck the Burin peninsula in 1929, causing considerable damage and loss of life. I wanted this band to be as big and as lethal as that wave: an unstoppable force of nature unleashed upon an unsuspecting public. We were all in. It was go great and go big... or go home.

Nineteen-ninety-five is a year I will never really remember, nor quite fully forget. We signed a deal with Warner Music and on September 12 we released our second full length album, *Up*, and immediately embarked upon a ridiculously ambitious, bone- and brain-rattling cross-country tour of Canadian university campus bars in a Dodge Caravan that my fifty-two-year-old body can still feel today.

It took a long time for the big-label promotional machine to kick in and most people outside of Atlantic Canada had never heard of us, so many shows were held at noon in college cafeterias where actual audiences were scarce and often bemused and even annoyed by our antics. Part of the problem was that many people simply couldn't understand what we were saying because we all spoke very fast in thick Newfoundland accents. Over time, we would have to learn to slow it down for the mainlanders. The evenings were generally spent just off campus in the local town bars, tearing it up for whomever we could get to listen. The pace was relentless but so were we, and there was no show we wouldn't half kill ourselves to get to for five hundred dollars and a case of cold beer.

We really didn't have a clue what we were doing, so we invested in our first professional tour manager to help keep our show on the road. Anthony Pitcher was just a few years older than us and also from St. John's. He was a part-time soundman from The Gasworks, an '80s hair-band bar in Toronto, and he reeked of weed and rock 'n' roll. Tony took control of the steering wheel every morning and manned the sound board at night and the band instantly got a lot quicker and a whole lot LOUDER. At $150 a day, he was the highest-paid passenger in the van, but he was worth every penny because he afforded us the time to focus our energy on improving our show and getting better as a band. He was also the best driver I have ever encountered. Over the course of ten years, two continents, and over three hundred thousand miles, we never had a single accident; and even though we averaged about 140 kmh, we never got a speeding ticket.

Bob Hallett always rode shotgun. The band may have been an equal partnership, but his seat in the van was never up for democratic debate; while we were in the vehicle, Bob always sat in "first class." I'm sure we all had days when we wanted to actually see where we were going, but Hallett was posessed of an unpredictable morning predisposition that nobody really wanted to fuck with, so the situation was just accepted as an unwritten rule.

Being in the front seat also gave Bob complete control over the van's radio and CD player, which was always turned off. Music, strangely enough, was not something we were allowed to share communally during the many thousands of van hours we punched in. At Bob's sole discretion, the consumption of new songs on the road would remain a solitary pursuit.

Darrell Power is Bob Hallett's complete opposite. Easygoing and always up for everything and anything, anytime and anywhere, Darrell was a constant source of entertainment to us all—except, of course, when he wasn't, which was usually in the early mornings while we sat waiting for him in the endless string of shitty hotel lobbies that helped harden our hearts out on that cold Canadian road. We may have been a party band, but our party ran with military precision and we were all very serious about being on time. Our attention to the clock was so fanatical that whoever was last to arrive in the lobby was still considered to be late, even if it was technically five minutes before the official lobby call. Darrell would often suffer the wrath of our angry words and dirty looks as he slowly gathered himself together in the morning, coffee in one hand, cigarette in the other, and the end of the previous night's last song still on his lips. His demeanor was so positive that all was usually forgiven within the first one hundred kilometres. What he lacked in dependability he more than made up for in goodwill. Darrell Power is a hard man to stay mad at for very long.

Alan Doyle is a narcoleptic extrovert with a very small bladder and a penchant for all things shiny. Blessed with the remarkable ability to command the attention of almost every audience (including one trapped inside a surly Dodge Caravan) and then fall sound asleep in virtually any position while moving, he is genetically predisposed to thrive in the unforgiving world of rock 'n' roll touring. His one weakness is his inability to hold his liquids for more than an hour.

Alan liked to pee as much as the rest of us liked to smoke Player's Lights. Every hundred kilometers was marked with a plea of "bustin'!" from the back and the van would inevitably have to pull over on the side of the highway so he wouldn't flood the back seat. Emergency roadside reliefs such as these were often on open ground with the van acting as the only screen. It was impossible for us to resist slipping the van into gear when his stream began and slowly rolling away, thus exposing Alan's "sprinkler system" to oncoming traffic.

All this time I was an alcoholic hiding from a secret, a lost boy looking for a way out. Even then I knew that singing drinking songs in the dirty bars of St. John's would end in one of two ways: disgrace or death—maybe even both. I had kicked around that too-small town long enough to see how that story ends. The clubs were full of damaged people like me. People who'd been hurt and were hiding from secrets and numbing their pain. Many defended themselves as "sociaholics" and somehow continued to survive one bad late-night decision after another. I saw the road as a means of escaping my own truth. Bombing down the highway with a bag of weed and a beer bash full of beautiful young women every night was an excellent way for me to defer reality indefinitely. As an alcoholic, being in Great Big Sea felt like winning the lottery, and I took full advantage of all the perks.

I can still drive for hours without stopping to pee.

No offence to all my brothers and sisters out there on the Prairies, but driving across the great provinces of Manitoba and Saskatchewan can be painfully boring, so we had to find ways to pass the slow-moving miles, and if there was ever an argument for using marijuana, it would have to be the obligatory eight-hour stretch of highway that runs between Winnipeg and Saskatoon. I remember scoring a large Mason jar full of prime BC bud from an agent in Toronto who wanted our business. It lasted us right through the mountains and took the sting out of many a lonesome mile. After imbibing, the inevitable munchies were never far behind, so we always kept a larder of Kit Kats and Miss Vickie's Sea Salt and Malt Vinegar potato chips on board to help level us out as the daily soundcheck approached. I remember an enthusiastic fan who owned a confectionary in Calgary giving us a huge case of Cadbury Creme Eggs for the road. I must have eaten a hundred over the course of that tour. I still have serious gastronomical issues with the Easter season as a result.

Back in the day we all smoked cigarettes, too, except for Alan who, after a few months, began to show signs of early-onset emphysema while trying to catch a few winks from his perennial perch in the back seat. One morning after a particularly bad coughing fit, Alan politely suggested that we all try to coordinate our inhalations so as to limit the damage we were collectively inflicting on his lead-singer lungs. It was decided that we would all smoke our cigarettes together with the windows open every half hour on the half hour. Alternatively, the Mason jar could be opened every hour on the hour for those who wished to avail of our "boredom coping mechanism." This all sounded perfectly logical to us at the time but it quickly became apparent that by sticking to a formal schedule, our actual consumption level would go up tremendously. As a smoker, you were afraid of missing an opportunity to light up so you ended up smoking every half hour whether you wanted to or not. We all started to sound like Leonard Cohen and look like Gordon Lightfoot and let's face it, unless you are in palliative care, a great big joint every hour for six to eight hours a day is probably just TOO MUCH WEED. By the time we reached Vancouver, the jar was empty and we were all as crispy as our delicious new girlfriend, Miss Vickie.

🍀

WE BEGAN TO try and "break" America in 1997 and brought on a second employee to help with the task. Danny Thomas, erratic bassist for the highly energetic but short-lived fraternal funk band Thomas Trio, was another veteran of the Newfoundland music scene. He was a hard worker with a big personality and an even bigger heart. If the van wasn't full before, it was well beyond capacity as soon as he showed up. He was so good at handling our instruments that I swear there were some nights he actually finished the show before we did. He was very efficient but often reluctant to accept any kind of constructive criticism. Adding songs to the set list was a non-starter. The show was over when Danny said it was over, regardless of whether there was a standing ovation demanding an encore.

At some point Alan thought it would look cool if Danny threw him his Takamine guitar from the side of the stage so he could catch it like a football. The visually impressive trick worked a couple of times, but we all knew this would eventually end badly...especially for the "football." Victoria, BC, was the last stop of the tour so we all began to celebrate a little earlier than usual that day. By the second set we were all feeling no pain until Danny launched "the Tak" a little early and a lot high. Time seemed to slow down as the great wingless, wooden bird drifted well over our heads and splintered against the far wall before landing as kindling on the far side of the stage.

Danny blamed Alan for not catching his touchdown pass.

I literally peed my pants a little bit onstage and it still makes me laugh out loud today.

Rock 'n' roll is a vicious game.

Red Wine and Whiskey

I'm a hard-working man
I am my father's son
If it wasn't for the liquor
I'd get a lot more done
You can take your gin and tonic
Take your Coke and rum
I'll drink red wine and whiskey
By the rising of the sun

Red wine and whiskey
Can lead a saint to sin
It's getting hard to draw the line
Look at the state I'm in
If you're looking for some trouble
I've always got the time
If you just bring along a bottle of
Good whiskey or red wine

Here's to all the girls who tried
To build a better man
To all the soldiers who have died
Back in Afghanistan
To the million tears my mother cried
'Coz she don't understand
Why I'd rather die of good red wine
With a whiskey in my hand

So crack another bottle
Raise another glass
Sling me one more shooter
Before I kick your ass
A dry life ain't worth living
The desert grants no ease
I'd rather sink into the ocean
And drink the seven seas

Red wine and whiskey
Can lead a saint to sin
It's getting hard to draw the line
Look at the state I'm in
If you're looking for some trouble
I've always got the time
If you just bring along a bottle of
Good whiskey or red wine

WHAT HAPPENS ON
THE ROAD...

GRADUATING FROM A MINIVAN to a tour bus means one thing to a live touring band: you have officially MADE IT. The year 1996 saw *Up*, our initial Warner Brothers release, sell platinum (one hundred thousand copies), which helped stabilize us financially and set us up for even bigger success for our seminal 1997 album, *Play*. Our music was resonating with people across the country and our raucous live shows had become a staple of both rock and folk music festivals. It took a lot of time and a ton of hard work but we were finally "living the dream." The vast majority of worthy Canadian troubadours never achieve this next level but somehow we survived the many hard-won miles spent crammed together in a Dodge Caravan for approximately two hundred shows a year from '95 to '99, and we were now more than ready to launch ourselves into the new millennium with some victory laps around North America in our ten-bunk rented Prevost.

There are two myths I would like to dispel right now:

1) Having sex on a tour bus is neither glamorous nor dignified. It's about as convenient as doing pushups in a phone booth.

2) Just because your bus has a toilet doesn't mean you are actually allowed to poo in it.

The Great Big Bus did remove the significant hassle of early A.M. lobby calls inevitably followed by extremely long and boring highway drives. Perhaps most importantly, arguments about when to pee and smoke would now be a thing of the past. Yes, life on the bus, though not as glamorous as we'd hoped, definitely made many aspects of touring easier—especially the consumption of alcohol. I can't think of a more convenient place to imbibe than barrelling down the highway in a bus with all your drinking buddies. It took us almost ten years, but by the time we finally earned our bus rights, we had arguably grown into Canada's biggest party band. Every night was Saturday night for us whether it was actually Wednesday in Winnipeg or Thursday in Thunder Bay. Our hard-drinking reputation wasn't undeserved and the party persona we promoted wasn't just an act. By now our daily show "rider" had also grown to real rock 'n' roll proportions:

1 bottle of single malt whiskey or Jamaican black rum
4 bottles of red wine (Australian and Californian)
48 bottles of imported beer (Stella or Corona)

Every day I went to work, this is what I would find on my "desk." I took my job very seriously and did my best to drink my full share EVERY. FUCKING. NIGHT.

Our after-parties were legendary and often spilled out of our hockey-rink dressing room and onto the bus after the rider had been demolished. Everybody wanted to have a drink with the boys from Newfoundland, and if you were a pretty young woman between the ages of twenty and thirty and showed up at our door without a boyfriend, your chances of getting on our bus were pretty good.

Tour buses can be configured any number of ways depending upon what the artists want. By 2001 we were a travelling force of ten including crew, so our options were limited to a central core of ten to twelve bunks bookmarked by a front and back lounge. The front lounge is where the kitchen and bathroom lived and, in our case, it was always designated non-smoking. The back lounge is where all the real badness happened.

In order to preserve "quality control" and increase our already incredible odds of sexual success, the crew were armed with special VIP "backstage pass" stickers and granted the liberty of applying them to the ladies they thought we'd like to meet after the show each night. The system worked well until one night in Guelph, Ontario, when the crew got a little "sticker happy" and ended up distributing over one hundred passes. When we came offstage, the dressing room was already full to capacity with gorgeous young women. Our scam was so blatantly obvious that a beautiful blonde walked right up to me and asked, "Why do I feel like a fish in a barrel?" Having exposed our philandering intent, the rightfully disgusted and disappointed female-dominated room quickly emptied and we were left to flirt with each other.

The back lounge continued to be a busy place, but after that embarrassment the special passes were abandoned and the crew's fishing license revoked.

The tour bus always came with a dedicated driver. These guys are a different breed to be sure, and we survived our fair share of racist speed freaks and rednecks with loaded guns. We had our favourites, but the good ones were always busy so you never really knew who you were going to entrust your life to for three to four weeks in a row, rolling up and down the highways of North America. Many a night my 2 x 4 x 8-foot sleeping space felt more like a coffin than a bunk, so I made well sure I was feeling no pain before I got horizontal and surrendered my body to the mercy of the road. Often, sleep eluded me completely and I would sit up all night with the driver, smoking cigarettes and staring at the endless ribbon of darkness as it rolled beneath our wheels.

One of those drivers was named Mikey. I never got his last name but Mikey hailed from Sudbury, Ontario, and drove for a number of reputable Canadian bands. Like me, he was never home. We pulled into a gas station late one night and, tired of our incessant daily deli tray, I decided (against Mikey's advice) to try a gas station cheese and bean burrito. It was a bad decision. Thirty miles down the road, those beans and cheese went to war in my stomach and I was overwhelmed with the sudden urge to evacuate my bowels. I informed Mikey of my situation and asked if he might pull over so I could poo, but we were at least another twenty miles from a gas station. He told me to hold it and I agreed to try, but after about ten minutes I knew the time for holding was over and that something would have to be done immediately.

"I can't wait anymore, man. I gotta use the toilet, Mikey."

"Please don't, Séan. We only have five more miles to go 'til we hit the next truckstop."

"Sorry, Mikey, but I gotta go NOW, man."

"Okay. If ya gotta go, ya gotta go, but please don't go right in the toilet 'coz it's broken and I'll have to get in there and clean it all out by hand. Take this Sobeys bag with you and dangle it under your ass when you sit down so your shit goes there instead."

I was in no position to argue.

I took the plastic shopping bag and headed for the tiny bathroom. As I crouched over the toilet bowl, I held the bag beneath my buttocks as directed and proceeded to fill it to the brim with toxic undigested beans and cheese. The smell was so bad it made my eyes water. The bag was so full I could barely tie it together to bring it up to Mikey, who was now pulled into a truckstop and waiting for me at the bus door. The smell hit his nostrils as I gently handed him the plastic bubble of brown hot mess and he bolted to the nearest garbage container where he dropped the offensive bag—and then promptly covered it up with his own vomit.

The shit people get up to in the middle of the night.

Long Road Lead Me On

This road is gonna be the death of me
Tonight may be my last
18 wheels and time to steal
There'll be no turning back
The highway is a hammer and I'm a rusty nail
Struck inside an iron mast and blown by diesel sails
It's a one-night stand, a heat without a heart
It's no man's land, an ending with no start

Long road lead me on... and on

A slick black ribbon wrapped round a widow's neck
A soul left unforgiven in a room full of regret
It's a ready-aimed rifle, a half-cocked loaded gun
And I'm gonna ride this bullet
Til there's nowhere else to run

Oh long road lead me on... and on

It's cold barbed wire cut through a desert frost
A funeral pyre, it's ashes unto dust
The silent surrender of breaking on black ice
This road is an altar
And I'm her sacrifice

Oh long road lead me on... and on

ABSOLUTION

ONE NIGHT WE got a strange request from our student promoter while drinking in our dressing room before a show at Acadia University in Wolfville, Nova Scotia.

"Father Johnny is here to see you. He's from Newfoundland and says he knows you guys. He's pretty cool. Can I let him in?"

None of us knew a "Father Johnny" but the decision was made to let him in for a quick hello just to be polite, and I was floored by what I saw walk through the door. Father Johnny was actually a former high-school hockey teammate and drinking buddy of mine. Back in the day, he was our on-ice enforcer and no stranger to a punch in the face or the penalty box. Now, all six-foot-four and two hundred and forty pounds of him was squeezed into a too-tight black short-sleeved shirt topped with a white plastic clerical collar that looked like it might pop off any second and take someone's eye out.

"Waddya'at, me old buddy?" He laughed as he lifted me off my feet and locked me into an uncomfortable bear hug.

"Jesus, Johnny! The last time I laid eyes on you, you were a bouncer at the Eager Beaver" (a strip club in St. John's notorious for its questionable local talent and frequent late-night brawls). "What the fuck happened, man!?"

"I got saved."

"Wha...? How...? And can you please put me down because I can't breathe."

He set my feet back on the floor and told me that he had had a vision of the Lord Jesus Christ late one night while he was tripping out on acid after his shift at the bar.

"He told me that He loved me and that He wanted me to become a priest...so here I am!"

I guess the road to heaven is easier to find for some.

We shared a drink and chatted until it was time to start the show. It was Saturday night and he said he couldn't stay because he had to say mass in the morning, so we wished him well and went on about our rock 'n' roll business.

It was a very LARGE evening that had not long ended when Darrell (my on-the-road roommate for eight years) and I were rudely awakened by a loud pounding on our Super 8 motel room door.

"Wake up, ye lazy bastards! It's time for mass!"

Sweet Jesus.

"Go away, Johnny."

"Come on, lemme in. I bought you some coffee...."

I was in pretty bad shape, but our lobby call was in less than an hour anyway, so I figured he was actually doing us a favour by bringing coffee; I got out of bed to let him in. When Father Johnny walked through the door his jaw almost hit the floor. The room was completely trashed. Empty booze bottles and beer bongs were scattered about, along with pizza boxes and buckets of chicken wings, overflowing ashtrays, and even a box of condoms and a hot pink bra for good measure. Nothing out of the ordinary for me, but not exactly what he was prepared for.

"So I guess you guys won't be joining me for mass this morning...?"

"I'd love to, Johnny, but I can't," I replied as I slowly emptied paper sugar packets into my Irving gas-station caffeine.

"You see, I haven't been to confession in almost ten years so I'm not in a state of grace and unworthy of the Eucharist."

"I can fix that for you right now if you like. If Darrell wouldn't mind stepping outside for a few minutes, I'd be happy to hear your confession."

"No offense, Johnny, but I don't think your ears are ready for what I'm carrying around. But I tell you what. If you use your divine power to grant me general absolution, I'll be the first one with my tongue out at the altar."

General absolution is a special dispensation to forgive penitents en masse, granted by the Church when Catholic souls are deemed to be in imminent danger.

By now, I was no longer a believer but I figured, why not?

Worth a shot.

"No, b'y. You knows I can't do that, McCann. If you wants forgiveness here today you're gonna have to spill yer guts just like everybody else."

Rules are rules.

I declined the invitation but kept the coffee and told my old friend to look me up whenever he got back home. Sure enough, just after Christmas the doorbell rang and there in his civilian clothes was my old friend, Father Johnny.

At the time I lived in a large turn-of-the-century townhouse in the posh east-end neighbourhood of Forest Avenue and had proceeded to fill it with a revolving door of live-in girlfriends who kept the place safe and sound while I was constantly away. At just thirty-five years old I had successfully paid off my first mortgage, a feat my father would not be able to match until he was sixty-five. I didn't own a car because I was rarely sober enough to drive. I had no debts and no dependents and was making money hand over fist, so I spent freely on frequent Friday night parties that often went on until Sunday afternoon.

The basement of my bachelor pad was cut from huge stone walls and covered in a cement floor. I got wrecked on acid one afternoon and painted the whole works bright red and called it the "Bucket of Blood." It looked like Dante's vision of hell but it was my favourite place in the world to get stoned, and I often hid down there for days on end playing cards, drinking whiskey, smoking hash, and listening to records.

I led John down into the Bucket of Blood and we cracked open a forty-ouncer of black rum, lit up some Player's Lights, and put on some Thin Lizzy. We kept the conversation light for the first five or six drinks, focusing more on the other Canadian religion: NHL hockey. As the night wore on and the distilled molasses continued to flow, we began to slur our way into matters more spiritual. John knew me when I was in grades eight and nine and he remembered how religious I'd been back then. Like many at the time, John knew that I had once considered the priesthood and asked me now why I hadn't followed through on my vocation. I liked Johnny, and after about a dozen Dark 'n' Dirtys I began to feel like I could trust him, so I decided to take him up on his offer to hear my confession.

"Forgive me, Johnny, for I have sinned and it's been fifteen years since I got fucked over really bad by a priest...."

I just blurted it out without warning. And with that, Father Johnny was hauling on his coat and heading for the door.

"I can't do this, Séan. I gotta get outta here...I gotta go home, man."

I guess he wasn't ready to hear my confession after all.

On the way out we passed the bookshelf where I now kept my copy of *Butler's Lives of the Saints*, with all its dark secrets hidden inside. If John wasn't willing to hear the truth, then I was determined to at least send it home with him. I stuffed the ancient books in a Sobeys bag and shoved them into the arms of the young cleric as he stumbled out my front door and into the cold, damp January night.

I haven't seen Father Johnny or the secret epistles since.

NEVER SAW IT COMING

♡

WHEN I MOVED to Vail, Colorado, my only intention was to forget all the family drama in Minnesota, to work as a waitress at a very busy restaurant to make some cash, and to do yoga as much as I wanted. I had done all of that and more in the year I'd been there. I'd grown, I'd healed, and I'd processed all the bullshit that had been weighing me down in Minnesota with family, the business, and my ex.

Through a year of hard work and introspection, I had allowed myself to reach into the scariest parts of my heart and soul and find out that I wasn't so broken after all. I was going to yoga every day in an attempt to find some peace. I was hiking and writing and enjoying all the beauty Vail had to offer a broken spirit. Alcohol, while still a tried and trusted friend, had started to take a back seat in my life to actually living a bit. I had begun to gain my confidence back, I had made some new friends, I was getting ready to move in with a roommate after my year of self-imposed "exile." I had re-entered the world of the living and was finally having fun again without guilt and fear.

It was about this time when I found out that one of my favourite bands, the Young Dubliners (the Dubs), was coming to town. I called up a friend and asked him if he could get me and my three girlfriends comped tickets. His only stipulation was that I had to go and thank Keith, the lead singer, for the tickets after the show. Easy enough, as there are only a handful of bars in Vail where the band could go after the concert.

What I didn't know about this particular concert was that there would be two other bands playing with the Young Dubliners that night. Bands I'd never heard of but which were clearly the same genre: Seven Nations and Great Big Sea. Whatever, we were there to see the Dubs because I'd promised my girls a great time and an even better after-party if we actually did find Keith.

The concert was amazing. All three bands performed to a half-full, but very appreciative crowd. People were dancing, clapping, and singing. It was a beautiful summer evening in the mountains and people were giddy, happy to be out in nature, listening to music, having some drinks. It was the type of atmosphere you hope for but rarely see at a concert anymore. No fights breaking out. No one jockeying for the best position in front of the band. Everyone was just really chill and relaxed but ready for a good time. The bands seemed more than willing to provide the musical backdrop to the pervading good-vibe sensation resonating throughout the amphitheatre. Seven Nations went first, then the Dubs, then Great Big Sea. Each band was better than the last.

As soon as GBS jumped out on stage, I noticed him. My girlfriends and I were standing stage right and he was stage left, but the band members all travelled around the stage so it really didn't matter. God damn, he was beautiful. While I was standing there with my tongue hanging out, staring like a fool, my friends started calling him "Mr. Yellow Shirt" because he was wearing a loose, faded yellow sweatshirt-type pullover. I honestly couldn't take my eyes off of him.

I want him, I remember thinking to myself. *I don't care if it's just for the night.* I am quite certain I wasn't the only person in that audience thinking that exact same thing.

My friend Michelle hit my arm as I was swooning over Séan and immediately started laughing at me. My friends had never seen me like this before. I didn't swoon. Ever. As a thirty-one-year-old in this mountain town of transients, I was ancient. As a divorcee and perpetuator of one bad relationship after another, I was way too old and jaded to swoon, and they all knew it. Plus, with the male-to-female ratio in Vail at 3:1, swooning was completely unnecessary.

Quickly, the desired effects of our strong drinks took over and I was dancing and laughing and drinking some more. By the end of GBS's set, the lead singer called for everyone to come up and join them, so we obliged! My friends and I, along with thirty other people, jumped up on stage and danced our asses off while the band played their last song. It was only later that I found out Alan's call was actually meant for the other bands to join them...not the audience. No wonder GBS had all been laughing so hard.

While dancing I only got within an arm's length of Mr. Yellow Shirt. He was jumping around, playing a sideways drum. I kept my eye on him the entire time, hoping for a chance to catch his eye. No such luck. Oh well, I was with my girls and we were having an excellent evening, so I just had to let the thought of Mr. Yellow Shirt go.

...STAYS ON THE ROAD

AT THE BEGINNING of the new millennium, Great Big Sea was firmly established in Canada but still struggling in the US and European markets. For ten years we had managed to sustain and survive a gruelling two hundred shows a year in an attempt to keep our options open and we were all starting to feel the effects. I remember having a sit-down with my bandmates to try and rethink our strategy and maybe lighten the mileage. After some debate, we decided to shelve our European pursuits and focus solely on "breaking" the US market. Distance was not really a factor. We all still lived in Newfoundland, so London, UK, was not much farther away than Boston. The real reason for our American refocus, though, had little to do with marketing. We had learned from years of experience that $150 could buy a lot more hotel room in North America, and we felt that by now we deserved queen-size beds and dependable toilets.

We had encountered several like-minded American acts out on the road over the many miles and it was decided that we should try pooling our resources in an effort to maximize our collective US audience potential. To that end, we enlisted the help of our California-based Irish friends, the Young Dubliners, and Floridian tribe, Seven Nations. The resulting Uprooted Tour went on for three months and was a complete failure in financial and career-building terms. It was also some of the most fun I've ever had in my life, and it was where I met the love of my life.

Vail, Colorado, was one of the final dates on the tour and supposedly a "Young Dub" stronghold. We had heard this many times before and the Dubs grinder, Keith Roberts, had a history of overpromising and underachieving when it came to actual audience potential, so our expectations were low for the beautiful mountain town. As it turned out, the show was a rare success, selling over three hundred tickets—a big number by Uprooted standards. Colorado was not our market to headline but by then it had become clear that we were the only one of the three bands with any kind of consistent fan base, so we agreed to close the show. At the end of our set, we invited the other bands to join us onstage and were surprised when the stoner ski bums in the audience thought the invitation extended to them. Everyone joined us onstage. It was a magical, marijuana-enhanced musical moment.

There were some very pretty girls in Vail that night and after the show I was determined to go out and meet one. As I walked out the backstage door, Keith grabbed me by the arm and led me to a waiting limousine, which proceeded to drive us both to a "private party" he had arranged at a local bar. This sounded like the perfect scenario to discover what kind of female companionship Vail had to offer, but when we arrived (three minutes later, because Vail is a very small town) I was shown into a room full of American fans eagerly awaiting my autograph and the new-but-already-annoying "selfie," which has since come to completely define audience-artist interaction.

It was an ambush.

As I waded into the fray and started signing CDs (remember those?), I asked how these fans had come to know that this was where I would be relaxing post-show. I was informed they had all paid an additional ten dollars for the opportunity to meet the band and asked when the rest of GBS would arrive. This was some shady side deal Keith had finagled with the local promoter to make some extra cash without telling us, and not something I would ever have agreed to. I have always hated officially manipulated "meet and greets" because they are superficial and insincere and leave most fans feeling cheated and underwhelmed. Paying an extra fee to meet me was just wrong. I was livid, and from the look on my face, Keith knew it.

"I'm so sorry, Séan. I shoulda told you the truth and I know you're really mad at me right now. What can I do to make this right?"

Over the previous three months on the road, this man had made me laugh harder than anyone else ever had, so it was impossible to stay mad at him for very long.

"I'm hungry and I'm lonely. Can you do anything about that?"

Keith Roberts is a man of great charm and innovation and a grinder of epic proportions. He sat me down at a table and two minutes later returned with the most beautiful woman I have ever met, and ten minutes after that he showed up with a pizza for us to share.

That woman's name was Andrea Aragon.

Bishop March, Funeral Mass remembrance card.

IN YOUR PRAYERS REMEMBER
The Most Rev. John March, D. D.,
Bishop of Hr. Grace, Nfld.
Born at Northern Bay, Nfld., July 13, 1863
Ordained priest at Rome March 16, 1889.
Curate at the Cathedral, Hr. Grace,
1889-1906.
Consecrated Bishop at Hr. Grace
November 4, 1906.
Died at Harbor Grace on January 12, 1940,
Interred at Harbor Grace
on January 16, 1940.
R. I. P.

Séan in London, England, grade 10, 1983. Photo taken by the priest.

Andrea skiing in Utah during one of many family trips; grade 10, 1987.
Photo by Jamie Aragon.

Ticket stub from Uprooted Tour concert in Vail the night Séan and Andrea met.

Note Séan left for Andrea after "one-night stand."

Séan visiting Andrea in Vail, Colorado, January 2003.
Photo by Michele Fischer.

Séan and Andrea shortly after Andrea moved to St. John's, late summer 2003. Photo by Chris Trapper.

Last day of XX tour with GBS, November 2013.
Photo by Andrea Aragon.

**Séan with fellow
survivor Paulie
O'Byrne, London
Recovery Breakfast,
September 21, 2014.**

Guitars for Vets concert poster. Drawn by Meaghan Smith.

Séan singing, sharing and surviving on Sexual Abuse Awareness day, February 5, 2018.

Séan finding his lucky charm, Anne Lise Boyer, in Newfoundland, 2014. Photo by Rani Majumder.

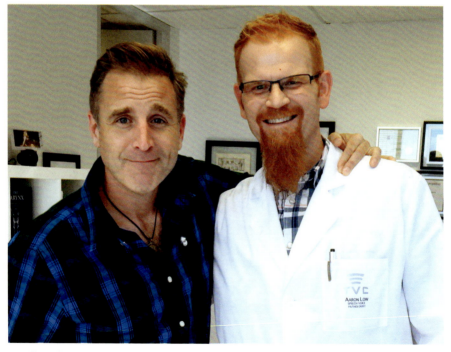

Feeling better in Toronto with healer Aaron Low, July 2016.
Photo by Katina Papaioannou.

The day Séan met Sheldon Kennedy and
they bonded over coffee and cake, spring
2017.

Clara and Séan, climbing mountains in November 2018.
Movement is medicine.

Séan and Andrea in late 2019.
Photo by Megan Vincent.

Séan, Andrea, and their two sons in late 2019. Photo by Megan Vincent.

IT HAPPENED SO FAST

♡

"I HAVE TO go thank Keith for the tickets; will you guys come with me to find him and then we can go to The Club and grab some more drinks?" Begrudgingly, the girls followed me into The Tap Room; due to its proximity to the amphitheatre, I figured it was the most likely bar the band would have chosen. I looked all over the first floor of the bar and saw no one from the Young Dubliners there. We then made our way up the steep, long staircase (at least it felt that way after the significant amount of alcohol I'd consumed) to the second floor.

In the middle of the second-floor bar was an enclosed glass room: a bar inside a bar. A voyeur's dream. The glass-encased bar allows everyone on the outside to see what's going on, but the "outsiders" are excluded from taking part. Perfect place for a band to have some of their fans and friends meet them for an after-party.

Just as I'm trying to figure out how to get us into the glass bar, I spot Keith walking by.

"KEITH!" I scream with vigour, because it's noisy and it's been over a year since I've seen him.

"Andy!" he yells back as he pulls me in for a hug.

"Thanks SO much for the tickets, Keith...it was a really fun concert!"

"No problem, Andy, glad you liked it."

I don't know if his brogue is thicker because he's drinking or if it's always been that thick and I just don't remember because I've been stone-cold drunk every single time we've hung out, but I'm finding it hard to understand him at all.

"Andy...come meet my friend in here."

"I'm here with my friends, Keith, can they come in too?" I ask.

"How many, and are they girls?" he asks back.

"There's four of us total and yes, all girls."

"All right then, come on!" And just like ducklings in a line (or lambs to the slaughter), we follow Keith into the room of glass.

Holy. Shit. It's MR. YELLOW SHIRT! And that's exactly what I mouth to my friends behind me. Of course we all start laughing, not one of us believing my incredibly good fortune.

The bar is loud and hazy from sweet cigarette smoke and there's a current running through the place that seems to make people vibrate with happiness. Oh my, up close Mr. Yellow Shirt is absolutely gorgeous. He's so, so beautiful and in total command of the people sitting around him and I can't help but stare.

Then, the bluest of blue eyes pierce me and I'm totally hooked.

"Andy, meet my friend Séan. Séan, this is my friend Andy. Here...have a seat right here, Andy. Séan, scoot over so she can sit down."

I am completely dumbstruck. I barely have words. I don't even reach to shake his hand, I just sit really really close to him...Mr. Fucking Yellow Shirt.

"You hungry?" he asks.

"Um, sure." At this point I'm unaware if I really am or not, but within three minutes a pizza from Vendettas (Vail's best pizza joint at the time) shows up in front of us. Seriously, a dude just put it down in front of us and said, "Here you go, Séan." I kind of chuckle when it happens, and I turn to him and say, "Really?" And so begins two hours of conversation. I couldn't tell you what we talked about. It really didn't matter; I just couldn't look away from him. Or his blue eyes.

After we've eaten the pizza, smoked some cigarettes, continued drinking barrels of wine, and talked our faces off, Séan leans in towards me and says, "Do you want to go someplace quieter?"

Ummm....yes please. "My place is just up the road from here, we could go there, unless you need to stay near your band, then we could just go to another, quieter bar."

"Your place" is all he says as he stands up, then holds his hand out to help me up.

I quickly give a wave to my friends. Clearly, they can see I'm leaving with Mr. Yellow Shirt and their hoots and hollers follow us out the door, down the now-treacherous stairs, and out into the crisp night air.

As we walk through the village, we make mundane small talk and I'm beyond nervous. Truth be told, I'd never had a one-night stand. Ever. Clearly I'm out of my depth because when he says, "I don't have any condoms, do you?" I actually start laughing. Like, full-on laughing. "Mighty presumptuous, aren't you?" I quip, trying to sound way more confident than I actually am. "Why else would we be going back to your place? To talk more?" (Insert a chuckle that shows no humour.) Okay, now I feel stupid. But he makes it up to me by grabbing my hand as we walk away.

The walking has helped me clear my head a bit, and I start realizing what events are about to take place. I'd be lying if I said I wasn't looking forward to getting my hands all over this man. I keep telling myself to play it cool. Except I have no idea how. This man has me so twisted up, I barely know where my apartment is.

We get there and are greeted by my surly but loving Kitty Cat. She's thirteen and has been an outdoor cat her entire life, but now has to live inside and incognito as pets aren't allowed in my building. Needless to say, she's constantly pissed and tonight's no exception. I don't think Séan's that amused at seeing her, but he gives her the obligatory scratch behind the ears and it's as if she's found a long-lost friend.

While I get us some wine, Séan sits in the living room and spies my guitar. It's a pathetically cheap thing, but I'd sworn I was going to learn how to play when I moved to Vail. I had learned three chords so far. Then he starts singing and playing. Bob Marley's "Redemption Song." Wow. Just, wow. His eyes are closed and he's singing like I'm not even there. There's so much feeling and sadness in it, my heart breaks just a little bit. It doesn't hurt my attraction to him either. Vulnerable, beautiful musician sitting on my couch, singing to me before we get sweaty in my bed? Yes, please.

We start to talk. He's clearly very drunk because he's going on and on about a friend he couldn't save. It's coming out as garbled and random and he's obviously upset about it so I'm trying to console him, but it's like I'm invisible, like he's talking to some ghosts who've settled in his brain.

Then he begins to ramble on about what a bastard God is and how evil God and priests and all of them are. "No one is holy. No one talks to God. You're not a direct line to God. What a fucking joke." He's in some kind of circular argument with himself. I try to break into his ranting and am mostly unsuccessful. He starts the cycle again, talking about how hard he tried to save his friend and how it didn't matter; God is a bastard, priests are evil, etc. I begin to worry a little bit, like, is this guy having a psychotic break or something? Or is he truly this tortured about whatever happened to his friend? Then I think, *Aw shit, this isn't going to happen is it? He's going to pass out on my couch and I'm going to have to go to bed with all this pent-up sexual energy.*

But then, just when I think all is lost, he looks up with me with those amazing clear-as-sky blue eyes and says, "Let's go to bed, sweetheart."

We walk the ten steps into my bedroom and he begins to take stock of it all. "All" consists of one queen bed, one desk, one very old computer, a second-hand nightstand with a single lamp and a book on it. Sparse would be an understatement. All my clothes fit into a 6 x 6-foot "closet" behind a curtain. The floor is so worn it's warped in places. The wood so walked-on it's smooth and slick if you're in socks. My bed isn't one of those made-up beds with forty pillows on it that are never used. Nope, it's very utilitarian. Two pillows, sheets, a blanket, and a comforter. Suddenly, as I'm feeling a bit embarrassed by my modest bedroom, Séan turns to look at me. His eyes are filled with nothing short of raw desire. It's a look I've long read about and seen in the movies but never in my life believed existed.

No words are exchanged. We both knew what we're there for, what we want, and what we need from each other. He grabs my hand and pulls me closer to him. He's got maybe two inches on me so I'm looking up into the deep ocean of his eyes. He smells of smoke, wine, and man. Musky, with a hint of lingering aftershave, mixed together in a heady combination that has my pheromones on high alert. I don't know that I've ever wanted this much in my entire life. Then he lays his lips on mine. They're so so so fucking soft. How can lips be this soft? But make no mistake, they are unyielding in their purpose. Our kissing quickly morphs into something deep, passionate, and unbridled. Before I know it, his hand is on the back of my head, turning it in just the position he wants. From that kiss, our bodies don't stop touching until it's time to get up.

I wanted to breathe him in and swallow his entire being. I wanted to crawl inside of him and stay. I needed us to be so intertwined that we couldn't tell where one stopped and the other started. In and of him. I wanted all of that and so much more.

We're a tangled mess on my bed. No clothes but legs and arms and hair all twisting together grasping in desperation like tonight is the only night we're going to feel this. It's as if we're both so in need of feeling something, anything, that we're determined to drag it out of each other. I know I'm scratching him. I can't help it. My nails dig long and deep along his back. I'm not trying to but it's egging him on. The more I scratch, the more insistent he is with his demands on my body. We're two pliable pieces of clay fitting in the right places, stretching, remoulding, and stretching again.

It was my first, and only, one-night stand.

The next day comes way too early. As a matter of fact, the night never really ended. There might have been a short nap in between our two bodies colliding again, but it never quite ended in sleep. I have to get up for work and Séan has to make it back to the bus. Then the hiding starts. My insecurity has taken hold and I run into the bathroom to dress and get ready for work. Never mind that this man has seen me naked and in various states of undress for the past nine hours, I'm embarrassed and shy and almost can't look him in the eye. He's just so beautiful, and I'm quite sure I'm never going to see him again.

I make the very short drive to the amphitheatre to drop Séan off at the bus. He says he'll call next time he's in town. (*How many times and to how many people has he said that?*, I silently wonder.) I awkwardly mumble, "I had a really good time," or something equally vacant, but really there's nothing else to say. We both know what this was and neither of us expected anything more. We share one last kiss before he gets out of the car—it's sweet and soft and very sad—and then he says, "Goodbye, sweetheart," and out the door he goes. I watch him saunter to his bus before I leave. He doesn't look back.

Once parked, I walk the four blocks to work and puke three times along the way. It's going to be a very long day but at least I have some delicious memories of an amazing night to carry me through. I wonder, as I'm on the threshold of the door of the restaurant where I work, if I will ever see this human again. Immediately, a feeling starts to take root in my brain, that this person and I are absolutely meant to be together.

I return from work later that night and get ready for bed. A bed that still smells like him, and I love it. I get ready to read the book that's been on my nightstand since I moved in, Joseph Campbell's *The Power Of Myth*, and on the inside of the front cover I see a message from Séan.

> I will never forget last nite
> You are an angel
> I will think of you often
> And see you again
>
> XO Séan
> (Mr. Yellow Shirt)

I cry myself to sleep that night.

HE SAID

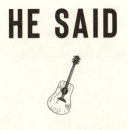

WHEN MY FUTURE wife dumped me at the bus the next morning on her way to work, I was completely destroyed. I'd survived many one-night stands over several years of serial monogamy but this was the first time I was ever sorry to say goodbye. I had even left her a note saying I knew that someday we would meet again.

"What happens on the road stays on the road" is an unwritten code followed by most travelling bands. The weekend after Vail, the Uprooted Tour wound its way to the Minnesota State Fair. I knew this was Andrea's hometown and was very excited at the prospect of seeing her again, even though I had a girlfriend living with me back home.

When you are looking into a crowd it's really hard to actually pick out a single face (especially when you're wearing whiskey glasses), and somehow I managed to miss Andrea's even though she'd made the sixteen-hour drive and was apparently standing right in the front row. Alan did see her but unfortunately failed to mention her to me until we arrived back at the hotel. The "code" had kicked in and he felt he was doing me a favour by sparing me a rematch with an old road flame. When I found out, I was distraught to have missed the girl I just couldn't stop thinking about. I hopped in a cab and spent the rest of the night driving around the Twin Cities, stopping at all the Irish bars (the most likely place to meet a shantyman post-show). My search was futile, and after blowing $150 in cab fare I found myself back in my Holiday Inn hotel room alone.

Why didn't I just call her? I did. But unfortunately, I had only kept her home number back in Vail, so I ended up leaving a very sad and desperate message on her answering machine (remember those?). Andrea couldn't call me because I'd been too much of a lying chickenshit to give her my own cell number. The code had to be respected and I was afraid of getting caught, so I went back to Newfoundland and tried to forget about my Rocky Mountain girlfriend.

SHE SAID

♡

IT BECAME VERY obvious to me after just a few short days that I had to see Séan again. I checked the Great Big Sea website and saw that the band would soon be in Minnesota playing at the state fair. At first I was worried there was no way he was going to see I was there if I went, because the grandstand is pretty big and the first row is quite a distance from the stage. But upon closer inspection, I saw they were playing at a small stage adjacent to the grandstand and I figured my chances were better at reuniting with him, so my decision was made and I was on my way back home.

On the night of the concert, I made it to the small area where GBS was playing a good hour before the show and parked myself right against the stage. I couldn't even tell you how the concert was because I was solely focused on Séan. I found myself at the opposite side of the stage to where he stood, but I didn't mind because when Alan gave me the old Newfoundlander wink and a nod, I was certain I'd be seeing Séan later that night.

When the show ended, the band went behind the stage curtain and the roadies came out to put away the equipment. I was confident Séan would soon be appearing from around that curtain to collect me, so I proceeded to patiently wait right at the front of the stage for a good twenty minutes after the concert was over. I finally asked their stagehand, Danny, if Séan was back there and if so, could he tell him that Andrea from Vail was here? Without missing a beat he informed me, "Oh, the band's already gone. They took a car right after the show and left."

What. The. Fuck.

Turns out Séan's right: what happens on the road stays on the road, and Alan, thinking he was doing Séan a solid, didn't tell him that the "girl from Vail" was in the audience, even though he later admitted to Séan that he'd seen me.

I had travelled all the way to Minnesota to see Mr. Yellow Shirt and was determined to find him, so I drove to every Irish bar in St. Paul that I could think of, but ended up back at my hotel empty-handed. As a last-ditch effort, I called my home phone back in Vail to listen to my messages, something I'd been doing constantly over the previous few hours. I felt certain that he'd seen me and just couldn't get to me, or that at the very least Alan would tell him I had been there after the show. Turns out, that's exactly what happened and Séan did leave me a message that night. He was drunk and he left me the most beautiful poem. I wouldn't erase it until several months later. But I remember it started, "You should have made your presence known and I would have stayed the night...."

Back home in Vail, I tried to get back into the normal swing of life. It wasn't too hard with work and yoga, but I couldn't quite get back into the social part of my world. I had no desire to meet anyone, and even going out with my girlfriends seemed a chore most times. After one particularly bad and boring night out I went home, turned on the TV, and started to watch an awards show. Being bored with watching fake stars, I went out to my deck to have a cigarette and look up at the real stars in the sky. I was so upset about not reconnecting with Séan, and I couldn't get him out of my mind. I had been absolutely certain I was going to see him again in Minnesota. Perhaps this was a sign that we were just not meant to be.

When you're in the mountains and it's dark, the stars are the street lamps. They are incredibly abundant and bright; you have no choice but to feel small. As I was looking up at the stars I asked my spirit guides out loud: "Am I supposed to be with Séan? Are we meant to be together?" Within one minute, a shooting star zipped through the sky. Seeing that shooting star was a sign for me. It told me that writing the letter that was in my head was the right thing to do at that moment. I had yet to decide if I was going to send it, but I needed to write it.

I went inside and wrote a six-page letter to Séan, pouring out my heart to him. I left nothing unsaid; I told him exactly what I wanted without fear of repercussions or embarrassment.

After writing the letter, I had to decide whether or not to send it. To be honest, I must have already made my decision, because after my first draft, which had scribbles and lines crossed out, I wrote another "clean" copy, so of course I was sending the letter. At that time I had a practice of writing things down, either in my journal or on a piece of paper, to get them out of me, to purge them. After looking at the letter for a day, I sent it.

I didn't have an address for Séan; all I had was the band's fan-mail PO box. So I went to the post office, got an express envelope, and sent my feelings and my heart off into the world.

And let myself hope.

A VERY UNLIKELY LETTER

THREE WEEKS AFTER finding, and then losing, Andrea, Bob and I were sitting in the Great Big Studio on the west end of Water Street in downtown St. John's when Alan walked in carrying a huge bag of mail. Over time, our physical fan mail had slowly been overtaken by email and online chat boards and we had forgotten all about the antiquated mailbox we continued to rent in the post office across the street. On seeing Doyle walking down the sidewalk, an astute and slightly overzealous postal employee cornered him outside with a huge bag of fan letters that had been accumulating for several years. We dumped the bag out on the studio floor and began sifting through its contents. About ten minutes in, Alan passed me a letter. It was addressed to me but it was already opened. He knew how disappointed I'd been when we left Minnesota. "I think you might want to read this one," he said.

I read it.

Then I walked around downtown and I read it again.

And then I walked back to the Bucket of Blood and broke up with my girlfriend.

Here's why.

Dear Séan,

It's been a week now since we met and I just returned from a mission to reconnect with a stranger who has recently occupied more of my thoughts than I would ever care to admit. I honestly thought you saw me Saturday night in Minneapolis but decided to forget you knew me. Had I known you didn't notice me there in the crowd, I would have stepped up but to be honest, I really have no idea how you would've reacted. Now as I sit here with my perfectly content cat, I can't help but regret my lack of courage. If given the opportunity, I will not make the same mistake twice.

Besides my father, you're the only person in this world who has called me by my real name. I like that. I like hearing you say my name. The impression you made has been seared into my mind; a precarious position for a girl who is fiercely independent especially since moving to Vail. I am at a point in my life where I have no patience for anything other than real, unabashed feeling. I live by that and truth be told, one day I will die by that. Honest, raw emotion is what lets me remember I'm alive. The utter joy and desperation you can feel is an experience like no other. I promised myself a long time ago to live with no regrets which is why I am writing you now to show you what is inside my heart.

I know I am not imagining the connection you and I felt and I know I'd do anything to spend more time experiencing that connection. Your entire being haunts me on a daily basis and, to be perfectly frank, I'm getting kind of tired of it. I am tired of being in a position where I can't delve further into my emotions to see if they're as real as I believe them to be... or imagined...and if they are real, then what the hell can I do about them?

I'm tired of perfecting my ego and my image. I'm tired of my life being something I just get through. I am ready to really live it.

Of course, if you are not where I am in my belief about the supernatural connection we had, well then I guess that's that. You can just put me in that "psycho fan" category you referred to the night we spent together.

If you are close to where I am in my mind then please know that I would desperately like to see you again. I want

*to spend hours talking to you and even twice that kissing
your face. I want to be naked again and feel you surround
my body like a warm blanket. I want to sit quietly and read
books with you. I want to see you through your own eyes and
for a little while longer, I want us to just be....*

*Séan, these things are not impossible. This world is a very
small place and yes, I just looked up Newfoundland on the
map....*

*I believe in this with my entire being. The question is what
do you want? Am I really on your radar or was I just an
empty "blip" on your screen? One way or the other, I feel I
need to know before I can move forward. Please just be honest with me, and for that matter, with yourself.*

*Whatever you choose, I would regret not telling you these
things. While your response could lead in one direction or the
other it's really secondary to the true purpose of this letter
which was to tell you what an incredible "blip" you have been
in my life and to thank you for that.*

*Either way, I sincerely hope this letter finds its way to you
and eagerly await your response.*

Truly,

Andrea

Bad things happen to everyone, but sometimes we get lucky and good
things happen too. The odds of me meeting my soulmate and future wife
in Vail were miniscule. The odds against her letter ever finding its way to
me in Newfoundland were astronomical. I took that as a sign that maybe
this was something meant to be, and for the first time in my life I decided
to listen to my heart. Along with eventually choosing sobriety, it was the
best decision I have ever made.

ROAD TRIP

♡

SÉAN CALLED ME on October 2, 2002, a little over a week after I sent my letter, and thirty-one days after that I drove the 2,200 kilometres from Vail, Colorado, to London, Ontario, to see him again.

The most vivid memory I have of seeing Séan that first time after our moment in Vail (and subsequent misfiring in Minnesota) is of him opening the door to his hotel room in London, looking me square in the eye, and saying with a wickedly sexy grin on his face, "Hello, sweetheart." He then grabbed me and hugged me like his life depended on it. He followed that up with the most searing kiss I've ever had. To this day it is most definitely the best kiss I've ever received.

After five days on the road with Séan (when I was only supposed to stay with him for the weekend), he said to me, "I'm madly in love with you. I've changed my entire world after Vail, after that letter." Followed with, "I need to be alone in the end, though." Of course all of this was said as we were a couple bottles of wine and whiskey in. That was the night we also started talking a lot about our histories. Family, work, previous lives. Séan was trying to describe Newfoundland to me because I knew absolutely nothing about it. As he did most times he was drinking (I would find out later in our relationship), Séan brought up the Church and the role it had played in Newfoundland and in his life specifically. All he ever said, until much later, was how fucked up the Church was, how he almost became a priest, how disappointed his mom was when he walked away from that path, and about the crazy priest who became a family friend who emotionally messed with his fifteen-year-old brain. I specifically remember thinking, during this particular conversation, how odd the entire scenario seemed. Having gone to a Catholic school, and having been raised Catholic, it was weird to me that Séan's family would have been so close with a priest. I knew my priests, but I would never have considered them family friends. I found it so odd that I ended up telling my sister about it when I called her from the road the next day, asking her out loud, "Do you think he was physically abused and just doesn't remember?'"

I should have listened to my instincts. I should have asked more questions. Or maybe it all went down the only way it could have in order for Séan to finally come to terms with it all those years later. But I do regret not pressing it more. I think, as with most things in life, you can't force someone to live their truth. They have to acknowledge it first, then want to walk through the fire of what that truth means in order to get to the other side. This is what Vail was for me, so I was intimately familiar with the struggle and pain of it all.

I remember showing up to Vail in the middle of the night and moving into an old, empty apartment as a completely broken person. I didn't have the courage to leave that apartment for almost a month, except to get groceries. It wasn't until I forced myself to get outside of that safe environment that I was able to begin to examine why I was so unhappy. I had to remember and think about all the crap I had been through leading up to my move to even begin to consider where I wanted to be in the future.

Revisiting the past to clear a path for the future is not necessarily a fun journey if you demand honesty from yourself. It is hard, scary, and most definitely painful. Perhaps that's why I didn't push Séan for more information early on. Unfortunately, that's a regret I have to live with, and I'll always wonder if maybe I could have saved us some unnecessary pain in the end.

I ended up staying on the road with Séan until the completion of that leg of Great Big Sea's Sea of No Cares Tour, which ended in Quebec City. I stayed a week and a half longer than either of us had anticipated, and as I said goodbye to him at the airport, I knew in my heart that I was going to spend the rest of my life with this man.

THE AGE OF ARAGON

AFTER A FEW very heated back-and-forths over the phone, it was decided that Andrea should join me on tour in Ontario to see if we were actually compatible. Instead of flying and renting a vehicle, Andrea decided to drive from Vail, Colorado, to London, Ontario—a solid twenty-two-hour drive. That she was prepared to invest so much time and effort into driving all that way just to see me did give me some cause for concern. We barely knew each other, so this seemed like an extreme gamble for a young woman to take in the poker game of love, but I was really hoping the bet would pay off for us both. She made it to my London hotel room just an hour before showtime.

"Hello, my love, I'm really happy to see you," I said as I held her road-weary body in my arms at last. "Thank you for coming—but we have to leave now."

Andrea had only seen Great Big Sea in front of a small Colorado crowd, so she was unprepared for the sound of nine thousand screaming fans when we walked into the loading bay of our sold-out show in London. The Great Big Machine was in full gear, with roadies and promoters running around everywhere, and she must have been wondering what she'd gotten herself into, but she handled it all with grace and composure. She watched the show from the side of the stage and I could hardly take my eyes off her. Who was this woman and what would become of us? I showed off for her as best I could but I really couldn't wait for the show to be over so we could begin to find out. I grabbed her by the hand once we finished our final encore and she and I slipped secretly out the stage door and back to our hotel.

Our long journey together had officially taken its second big brave step.

Initially, the plan was for Andrea to just stay for the weekend, but we hit it off so well that we just couldn't say goodbye again so soon. We decided to prolong our date as long as possible and I jumped into her Nissan Xterra for the remainder of the Ontario shows. When they were over, we still weren't finished with each other and drove our burning romance on to Montreal and finally Quebec City, the last date on the tour. I had developed a network of steady road flames over the years, but that house of cards came crashing down as the tour rolled on, and I was deeply saddened when Andrea and I finally had to say goodbye. When she dropped me off at the airport in Quebec City in late November, we agreed to meet again in Vail after the Christmas holidays.

As I boarded a plane for Newfoundland, Andrea began the 3,300-kilometre, 32-hour drive back to Colorado. *This woman is either completely nuts or she must really love me*, I thought.

Maybe it was a little bit of both.

We spent the month of January 2003 holed up in Andrea's small apartment in Minturn, Colorado, just getting to know each other better...feeling each other out. We'd both been in long-term relationships before that had failed spectacularly and we really wanted this one to work. We had also both learned by now that *work* is exactly what real relationships require. We took our time and talked a lot and we let our love grow stronger as we snuggled together in our frozen mountain hideaway.

Parting this time proved even more painful, so before we said goodbye we made a plan to spend another month together on the Hawaiian island of Kauai six weeks later. I believe you don't really get to know somebody until you've travelled with them. I wanted to commit completely to this relationship, and this trip, in my mind, would be our chance to play our last hand. It was time to either hold 'em or fold 'em.

The plan was to meet in San Francisco, spend a few days walking around seeing the sites, and then fly straight to Kauai, where I had rented a vacation home just outside the small village of Kapaa. Andrea checked into our hotel in San Francisco the day before I arrived, and when I walked into our room she was wearing a very sexy pink jumpsuit with a zipper running down the length of the top. I was well pleased with what I saw and instantly proceeded to unwrap my present. As the zipper slowly rolled down revealing her long, beautiful, naked body, I was surprised to see a name spell itself out across her chest one letter at a time:

SÉAN

There I was, emblazoned on a lotus flower and burned across my lover's heart forever. If I had any lingering doubts about Andrea's devotion to me, they were destroyed completely right there and then. My long search for genuine love was over. It was time to start building our home together.

WE BEGAN MAKING plans for Andrea to move to St. John's while we were still on Kauai. We didn't know what she would do for work but we were now certain that we were meant to be together. The big questions had been answered. The small ones would eventually look after themselves. Andrea hadn't even heard of Newfoundland until the night she saw our show in Vail, so I expected there might be some degree of culture shock for a Minnesota mountain girl suddenly moving her entire life to "The Rock."

Andrea landed in typically high winds with all her worldly possessions and her fifteen-year-old cat, Kitty, in May of 2003 and I picked her up in a new Honda Element I'd purchased especially for her arrival. I hadn't bothered to own a car in years because I was seldom home and rarely sober enough to drive. Americans love their automobiles and Andrea is no exception. I felt it was the least I could do after the thousands of miles she'd initially logged to light a fire under our new relationship. She wasn't much impressed by my vehicular decision but really seemed to enjoy living in my spooky old mansion and drinking with all my wild friends in the Bucket of Blood.

Newfoundlanders have a tendency to speak quickly, and many still wear thick accents, so I spent a lot of time trying to translate for her. My friends took a quick liking to Andrea, for the most part. Charming and good-looking, she was an easy sell for the men, but some of the women were suspicious of this foreign invader and a few were downright rude.

"Why'd you have to go and hook up with an American girl? Newfoundland girls not good enough for you anymore?"

To which I would always reply, "I just wanted to find someone that none of my buddies had already slept with."

And I wasn't even half joking.

PART III

PROVERBS

NOT WHAT I EXPECTED

♡

WHEN I MOVED to Newfoundland, Séan and I were on a whirlwind romantic tour of life. We had been in a long-distance relationship for the past year, with extended visits to each other's houses, and a luxurious month in Hawaii. It was perfection. We'd only met a year prior, and here I was moving to the end of the world (in my frame of reference anyway). In moving to Canada, I'd depend solely on Séan financially and socially. He would be my family. That's a pretty tall order for someone who would be gone more than he was home.

The first year in St. John's was good. It was great fun having no responsibilities, to go out drinking all night, get up at noon or later, laze around all day, and then do it all again the next night if we wanted. In St. John's you were never hard up to find someone out or going out. We never had a problem having people meet up with us or come over to the house for drinks and chats. We were always drinking.

Whenever he could, Séan would take me on tour with him. I saw so many parts of Canada driving hotel to hotel and venue to venue with him. It was our own slice of rock 'n' roll (well, folk 'n' roll) fun. We already knew we travelled well together, and I had no problem catering to Séan's many moods while on the road because I was thrilled just to be with him. The party truly never stopped on tour. Just like when we were back in St. John's, we'd sleep until we had to drive to the next town, get settled in the hotel, eat something, go back to our room, and make love; Séan would nap, I would get ready, and then it would be time to go to the venue. Our night ended with many drinks, many cigarettes, and lots of laughing. We'd get back to the hotel room, have a few more glasses of wine or whiskey, make love, then fall asleep exhausted and happy, ready to do it all again the next day.

It was perfect and fun and completely, absolutely without responsibility. Life back home in St. John's wasn't much different. It was all great fun... until it wasn't.

Living with someone is hard enough. Living with someone with an alcohol problem is like being trapped on a merry-go-round of emotions. Never would I have thought I would live with not one but two functioning alcoholics in my lifetime, yet here I was.

Even more tragic is that I loved both of these alcoholics so much that I put myself at risk for the sake of being in their orbit. I love my dad, and I love Séan. Deeply. Those loves almost killed me emotionally and physically. I allowed their pain to be my pain. I accepted being their emotional punching bag when they were drunk, and I took all of that pain, theirs and mine, and allowed it to manifest physically as everything from stomach ulcers to insomnia.

When Séan would travel out of the province without me, I would get my downtime (dry out and sober up) and be more than ready to go out when he came home. Problem was, as time went on, I started not to be able to keep up with Séan's drinking when we did go out, so that meant I would usually come home alone. I simply couldn't keep up with him and his seemingly insatiable thirst. I always knew when it was time to go home; Séan never had that off switch. I should have been concerned. I should have seen it as a problem, but it only became a problem when I couldn't and didn't want to keep up with his pace anymore.

One such night, after a full day of drinking, we finally make it home and Séan opens a bottle of wine. It's going on 11 P.M. I'm just happy to be home so I sit in front of the fire and drink wine with him. As of late, a reoccurring theme Séan brings up when he's drunk is either the people in his life who've left him or, again, how fucked up the Catholic religion is. I liken it to when I was drinking with my dad and the conversation inevitably turned to people who had fucked him over in business, or Vietnam. I don't know why it's taken me well into my forties to understand that this is a THING. Not talking about something when sober then constantly bringing it up when you're drunk means it's an issue. Hindsight is so very 20/20.

During Séan's diatribe about an old friend he'd given piles of money to, someone whom he says he was a "saviour" to, he quickly switches his focus to the family friend who was a priest. His sentences at this point are meandering at best, but he manages to explain that this priest befriended him, took him to Europe, then played mind games with him once Séan decided he didn't want to go into the priesthood. He's full of venom and vitriol and is throwing verbal punches at a demon I can't see and certainly don't understand. But it is at this point in our relationship, during this very drunken and fucked-up night, that I realize the priest did more than verbally abuse Séan. And so, I ask him: "Are you certain there wasn't any physical abuse?" With absolute certainty that only a drunk can give, he scoffs and says of course he's certain.

I finally cajole him upstairs at 1:30 A.M. and as he proclaims how incredibly bombed he is, I know sex is off the table. And for that, I'm grateful. I just want to get him into bed (safe) and passed out (safer). These are the depths to which I've sunk in thinking about what a safe night drinking with Séan looks like: him passing out. But when I assure him we're not having sex and I can't wait to go to bed, the ugliness comes spewing out at me.

"I can take a hint!" he seethes at me. He turns his back to me in the bed, then proclaims he's wide awake and needs to do something, go somewhere. He proceeds to get up and get dressed, and I start to panic. I panic because I know how incredibly drunk he is. I know he's not in possession of his faculties and I know he could get very hurt if he goes out again. I'm afraid. I'm afraid for him and for me. I'm definitely afraid for us. I hear myself start to whine to him about why he wants to go and where he's going to go—it's after 1 A.M., afterall. As I hear myself and my whiny voice, I wonder what the hell happened to me. When did I become this girl?

It's not the last time I'll wonder that.

If you've never fought with a drunk, you can't possibly know how exhausting it is. In reality, you probably shouldn't even *try* to fight with a drunk because there is no such thing as logic in a drunk person's mind. But I wasn't about to let Séan go downtown to get more drunk. The fight lasted probably forty-five minutes—although in truth, it's a fight that lasted eight years.

During these fights, I'm always sober, even if I start out tipsy. By the time we get to the fighting phase, Séan has been drinking for hours and I've long since sobered up. That means I have the luxury of remembering everything. I get to remember his twisted, snarling face when he gets angry at my insistence he's had enough. I get to remember the veiled threats of how my insecurity is going to push him away. I get the joy of remembering how he compared me with the groupies who'd love to be having sex with him while I won't. I'm left reminded of how vast our financial inequity is, how much I'm given. Lucky me, I get to remember every last detail.

And the drunk gets to remember nothing.

When you don't remember anything, you have nothing to apologize for.

As expected, the next morning Séan doesn't remember anything after leaving the bar. I remember everything, and still feel the sting today.

HOW BAD COULD IT BE?

EVENTUALLY WE FOUND our local social focus and Andrea settled into her new St. John's lifestyle, which generally meant she was home alone most of the time. The band continued to tour successfully throughout North America and I was understandably expected to show up for work regardless of my new relationship status. Business was good and the band generally got along well enough to survive in the iron bubble of the bus. The road was still a place far removed from our domestic worlds, a place where we could focus on song creation and find consensus on how to keep moving forward. It was often lonely but at least we had each other.

St. John's was a very long way from Andrea's world—it's a long way from just about everywhere—and I knew she was finding it hard staying home alone with her cat while I was away. Then one night as I arrived home really late from the airport and tried to sneak into the house without waking her up, I was attacked on my own porch by a small, furry, four-legged animal who tried to crawl up my leg and then pissed all over my boots. Andrea had gone out and gotten herself a roommate.

Marley was the first pet I ever owned (Kitty was *all* Andrea's). There'd been a few hamsters as children and my mom got a lapdog just before I moved out, but this was a full-on and for-real dependent. Another living thing was about to enter my super self-absorbed life and I wasn't sure If I was ready for that.

"Do you like him?"

It was obvious to me that Andrea was worried I might suck as a parent and Marley was really a test to see if I was a viable future father to her children.

"Does he always pee on people when they come in?"

"Only the people he really likes. I think he likes you a lot."

Marley was a rescue dog who suffered from severe separation anxiety. It got to the point where we couldn't leave him in the house alone, so Andrea and I sat down to consider our options.

"I guess we'll just have to bring him back," I said hopefully.

"Don't be silly, Séan. We will simply have to find him a best friend."

"Dear Jesus...."

I found Marley's best friend two weeks later in a basement apartment in the city's west end, another freeloader we named Tosh. My life was now full of other living things and after a few months my surly old self actually began to like it. What I didn't realize at the time was that this was all just a test. Andrea, in all her wisdom, had much bigger plans for us.

Just short of Marley surviving his first year on Forest Road, Andrea asked me what would eventually prove to be a very loaded question.

"How do you feel about babies?" she asked quietly as we basked in the post-coital glow of an afternoon delight.

"I think they're stupid," I replied facetiously. "They shit themselves and they don't even know how to talk."

"Come on, Séan, be serious for a second. Have you even thought about us having a child?"

"No...but I am beginning to think that you have, right?"

"A lot. It's just such a huge responsibility and I don't know that we're ready. Do you think I'd make a good mom?"

"I think you'd make an excellent mom, Andrea. You love lost things and look after them, like the dogs, and like me."

"Do you want to have kids, Séan?"

"No...but I wouldn't stand in your way if it were really important to you."

"Is that a yes?"

"It's a qualified okay. I mean it's just a baby, not a bomb, right...so how bad could it be?"

I would learn exactly how bad it could be less than a year later, on October 11, 2005, when I waited anxiously for Keegan Cash to leave his mother's body and fill his tiny lungs with air for the first time. Andrea's labour was going reasonably well until Keegan changed his mind and decided at the very last minute that he would prefer to remain inside. The top of his head was actually visible, so the doctor decided the best course of action was to monitor the baby's vital signs until Keegan was ready to finish what he'd started. After about an hour, Keegan's vital signs began to drop and emergency measures were taken to literally drag my first-born son kicking and screaming into this cold world. For his first few seconds in daylight, I swear I could see right through him. He looked like a tiny alien, all pale and translucent, eyes black as a country road at night. As I held him, I began to fully realize the great responsibility we had taken on and how much our lives would be forever changed.

This was no bomb. This was something far more powerful.

Before I passed him back to his mother, Keegan's tiny hand wrapped around my little finger and I felt my hardened old heart be quietly blown apart. I have been wrapped around his little finger ever since.

THE MORE THINGS CHANGE

♡

ON DECEMBER 24, 2004, Séan proposed. I wasn't expecting it at all. It was Christmas Eve and we were having a party for a handful of friends who had no place to be. I had unsuccessfully been trying to cook a prime rib roast while managing drinks for our guests, who included a chef with a broken hand, hopped up on painkillers and booze. It was controlled chaos. After finally calling "uncle" on the roast, I sat down in our living room with its roaring fire and basically chugged two glasses of wine, desperately trying to catch up to the buzz of the partygoers around me, especially Séan.

I remember him sitting right next to me on the couch and looking at me bleary eyed—he'd been drinking for a few hours at this point—and grabbing my hand.

"You know much I love you, right?"

"Yeah...what's up?" I was exhausted and pissed at my lack of cooking skills and really in no mood to talk to drunk Séan.

"I just need you to understand how much I love you."

"Yes, Séan, I understand. What do you need?" Even *I* know I'm being bitchy at this point. Then he clumsily slides down to one knee (I still haven't clued in to what's about to happen because I say, "Get UP! What are you doing?!")

"Andrea, would you make me the happiest man on earth and marry me?" He holds open a box with a ring that can only be described as my personality in platinum. Then, complete and total disbelief. Shock. Mouth agape.

"What? Are you kidding? Really? Yes!"

I didn't step foot back in the kitchen the rest of the night and have no idea how we ended up feeding all those people.

Throughout our short relationship to this point, Séan had been more than vocal about not wanting children. Outright hostile is more like it. He'd travelled the world and he knew children only as the very loud, disruptive beings on his flights. But in early February 2005, I was in the parking lot of Sobeys after taking three pregnancy tests, crying to my sister about having to tell Séan I was pregnant. I was considering all my options; I was panicking. I could tell him and we could deal with it together, I could leave him and go to Minnesota and tell him nothing, or I could terminate the pregnancy. I'd kind of always known I wanted children—I loved my nieces and could see myself as a mom eventually—so terminating my pregnancy wasn't really an option for me. But I was terrified. I was terrified of Séan's response because I knew how strongly he felt about not having kids. I also knew how much a child would change the way we were living our lives. I knew that I, for one, couldn't be out all night drinking and smoking. I knew I was going to be tired and crabby and have another human to put first. I knew the party was going to end, or at least become less frequent and a lot tamer. And as much as I knew these things, I knew Séan was in no way a fan of ANY party EVER ending.

Much to my surprise, when I told Séan, he was fantastic about it. Truly. He was shocked but happy-ish. I was relieved to find out termination wasn't an option for him either, but I quickly found out life would be changing more for me than it would for Séan.

And it stayed that way for the next six years.

During my pregnancy, Séan's favorite line was, "We won't have to change much, it's not a bomb, it's just a baby!" He wasn't wrong, because the reality was that nothing much did change for Séan. Nothing had to. I was well versed in keeping him happy when he was home. I had been playing this peacekeeper/happiness-provider role ever since I was young and I'd had to deal with my dad. I knew how to keep the beast of alcoholism sated and under control. I think they call that an enabler. However, Séan's beast, his alcoholism, was far bigger and stronger than I was used to—or should I say, stronger than I wanted to admit.

There were many times throughout my pregnancy when I started to question how big an issue Séan's drinking was. It started out as a little niggling feeling of *Hmmm, maybe this is a problem*, but eventually turned into a *Holy shit, what do I do now?*

Having Séan partying at our house with a very dear friend until 4 A.M. when I was four months' pregnant should have given me pause, but that was easy to justify. Although this person lived in St. John's, Séan rarely got to see him. *It's fine*, I thought, *it's a one-off situation*. Constantly going out or staying out when I was home, then not making it back to the house when he promised he'd be home, should have been a warning sign. Or maybe the time Séan brought home a man (a stranger to me) who had just assaulted his wife so he could introduce me before he took the guy to rehab should have caused me some serious reflection, but no, it did not. Every time I should have stuck my hand up and yelled, "HEY! SOMETHING'S NOT RIGHT HERE!" I remained silent. Rocking our very precarious boat was not something this coward was willing to do.

On June 23, 2005, Séan and I stopped working on our makeshift nursery and headed with our two close friends down to the courthouse to get married. We were in our painting clothes and honestly had not put much thought into the process. I actually had no intention of ever getting married again since my last marriage had been such a complete failure, but in the advent of new cross-border security due to the events of 9/11, I knew travelling with the baby inside my belly was going to be much easier if I was married to the father and the baby had our shared name. So basically, I convinced myself this marriage was a means to an end. A technical detail necessary for me and the baby to go visit my family. In hindsight and in truth, this marriage was a promise of love, loyalty, and devotion I was looking to keep and have kept, for once in my life.

The judge kept asking us if we were aware that the proceedings were legal, and if we were sure we wanted to do this. Apparently showing up for your legal marital proceedings in painting clothes is off-putting to a judge. But he married us and signed the paper, so legally wed we were.

On July 1, 2005, just over a week into our marriage and three months before Keegan was born, Séan proclaimed to me: "That's it...I'm not drinking anymore." On July 11, 2005, Séan stumbled in the house drunk at 4:50 A.M. It was at that moment I started planning how to raise a child as a single mother. I had asked Séan to start cutting back and to not go out or drink as much and he had clearly made his choice in the matter.

On July 25, 2005, Séan and I, along with our families and close friends, celebrated our marriage with a "ceremony" performed by his aunt, a nun. It took place in our house and lasted maybe twenty minutes. But in that time, Séan thanked God twice for me, which I found odd and very awkward, considering he never spoke of God in favourable terms. Pictures from that day, before, during, and after the ceremony, show how much pre-partying was going on while I was getting ready. By the time the actual reception started, there were fewer than ten of us (three of whom were kids) who were actually sober. I am quite certain Séan has very little, if any, memory of that day.

On October 11, 2005, the night following Keegan's birth, Séan proceeded to get very very drunk with a friend of his back at our house. My sister, staying with us to help out, had to wake him up the next day so he wouldn't sleep through visiting hours. On their way to the hospital, Séan had a very close call with a pedestrian as he was basically still drunk. My sister still doesn't let him drive her anywhere.

Anyone who has children will tell you they can be hell on a marriage. Relationships are hard, this I know. But add to that taking care of a baby, and the relationship falls by the wayside. I definitely wasn't good at multi-tasking those two responsibilities. Séan was amazing with our baby, but our relationship was strained to say the least. We were basically roommates. When he wasn't with Keegan or on the road touring, Séan was either out or having drinks with friends at the house. He had an outdoor fireplace made specifically so he could be outside with his friends in the summer (and winter, if the snow wasn't too deep). The number of times I'd actually have to go out to the fireplace and tell his friends to leave and Séan to come in and go to bed were too numerous to count.

I knew Séan absolutely adored his baby, but beyond that, I knew he wasn't happy. I just figured it was me he wasn't happy with, that he had decided marriage and babies weren't his thing. And I started to doubt his desire for me. During this time I wasn't going out with Séan at all so I wasn't subjected to his drunken rants and ramblings. Mostly when he came home he would go into the guest room and Keegan and I wouldn't see him until at least noon the next day.

Séan didn't have to leave for me to become a single parent. He was just one moving mass of utter unhappiness. When he was home from tour, he was unhappy; when he was on the road, he was missing home and unhappy. Only being with Keegan gave him some joy and some peace, but it's not like he was with Keegan a lot of the time, because while it brought him joy, a baby, as we discovered, is hard work.

The night before Easter Day 2008, Séan decided to go out. I was two months away from giving birth to our second baby, Finnegan. Keegan was two-and-a-half and the relationship between me and Séan had deteriorated so much by this point that I didn't even really protest his going out anymore. I was sick of fighting a fight I knew I wasn't going to win. He'd left the house the previous night saying he'd be home by midnight. When midnight passed and I called him, he said he'd for sure be home by 2 A.M. When I called him at 2, there was no answer. Finally, at 5:53 A.M., I heard Séan stumbling into the house.

As I'm standing at the bottom of the stairs by the front door, he blurrily looks at me. "Yeah, I know it's late."

"Late?! It's fucking 6:00 in the morning! That's tomorrow!"

"Is it really 6:00?"

He's slurring and stumbling, trying to get up the stairs to bed. I breeze past him and say, "You're a fucking piece of work." I close our bedroom door as there's no way in hell he's sleeping in my bed. Keegan wakes up half an hour later.

The most vivid memory I have of that day isn't Keegan running around the house and backyard looking for eggs, it is of Keegan going into our guest room where Séan was sleeping because he was excited to show Daddy all the fun stuff he'd just done. It was 10 A.M. and I let him go into the room thinking Séan would at least pretend to rally. All he did was roll over. I told Keegan Daddy was very tired and we'd try again in a bit. Two hours later, Keegan, who was now desperate to see Dad and tell him all his stories about what the Easter Bunny brought, ran into the room saying,

"Daddy, Daddy, come on get up now! You have to see all dis!" Again, Séan didn't get up. Séan managed to get up at 2 P.M., after all the Easter activities had passed. That day, he broke not just my heart but Keegan's, too. I vowed right then and there I was going to change this situation. I started thinking about how I could run away (my specialty) back home to Minnesota. But my promises to leave or kick him out were as empty as Séan's to quit drinking. Even more so, in fact, because I never once said the words out loud. I guess we were both utter failures at living a truthful life. What an example we were showing our son. My god, we were so utterly broken.

Although Séan never once put his hand on my stomach when I was pregnant with Finn, our little featherhead was born with little incident, a ridiculous head of hair, and a big scream. I gave birth to Finn on a Saturday afternoon. Five hours later, Séan was at a local St. John's bar, the Sundance, for a GBS corporate show. He left us at 4 Saturday afternoon and I didn't see him again until Sunday evening, even though the event, our house, and the hospital were all within a five-mile radius.

Not much changed in our exhausting relationship over the next couple of years. I was overwhelmed with two small children and a husband who was gone more than he was home. And when he was home, other than spending time with the kids, he was absent to me. For Séan's part, he seemed to get more and more angry and despondent as those years wore on. I couldn't understand it and of course I thought it was all about me. I thought it was a manifestation of his desire to not have a marriage or a family weighing him down anymore. We weren't talking much beyond having discussions about the kids, and when we were together and the kids were being watched by his parents, we were usually drinking and not talking about anything. We were just existing with each other. It was horrible.

There were a few times we'd try to rekindle the flame that once warmed us both, but it always ended disastrously. One thing about Séan and me is that we never did anything halfway: if we were going to love, we loved hard; if we were going to fight, we fought harder. Between the loving and fighting, drinking and avoidance became our coping mechanisms.

SLOW LEARNER

LOOKING AFTER A brand new life brought with it a steep learning curve and no shortage of new stress, but we tried our level best as parents to do no harm. I think we did okay for first-timers and Keegan grew quickly and with relatively few issues. He started asking for a little brother to play with as soon as he could talk, so Finnegan Fuego would complete our family just two and a half years later. There were, of course, a lot of dirty diapers to deal with but we had a lot of fun, too. I was still on the road a lot so Andrea did all the hard work, and mostly by herself. Even when I was home, I found it hard to adjust to the mundanity of daily life with small children and often found myself taking the edge off in the evening with a bottle or two of red wine after they finally went to bed. Sometimes Andrea would join me, but most nights she was just too exhausted to stay awake and fell straight into bed.

Our social life, which only a few years earlier could accurately have been described as extreme, was now just a postcard memory, and our sex life was simply non-existent. I began sleeping in the spare room so as to avoid waking anyone up when I came up late to bed and to escape being woken up by crying babies from my own wine-buzzy sleep. I was constantly restless and quick to anger over domestic issues. The best part of my days was spent traipsing over the White Hills above Quidi Vidi on the east end of St. John's with my boys and dogs in tow. Sometimes we'd light a fire and roast some wieners. Other times, we would build a lean-to out of spruce boughs and old rope. I never felt anxious while walking through the woods and I don't think the rest of the animals did either.

When I was gone on tour I was really gone, so I tried hard to spend time with the boys when I was home and give Andrea a break. But home for me was hard because it didn't afford me the unlimited access to alcohol I had grown dependent on for almost twenty years. I may have been a new father but I still had an old secret to keep. I hadn't made any attempts to face my truth or deal with my past. My problems were all still in there, eating away at my insides, waiting to explode. Alcohol was my only coping mechanism, and removing it from my personal defenses while raising my stress with the responsibilities of parenthood was bound to end in disaster.

And eventually it did.

THE ENEMY INSIDE

I HAVE TRUST ISSUES.
Being sexually assaulted by my priest as a teenager left me with deep emotional scars that are still healing even today. To be so betrayed by someone I believed in completely was a blow I have never really been able to bounce back from. This man was more than just my priest. He took great interest in me when I was vulnerable and quickly became my closest companion, even though he was more than twice my age. In less than a year he had basically moved into our home, and I looked up to him like an older brother. Because of what happened, my adult life has been wrapped in a blanket of suspicion and doubt. I suffer from social anxiety and often find it difficult to be around people. This may sound strange given my chosen occupation of performing publicly in front of thousands, but I saw the stage as a place where I could be protected within the safety of the crowd without actually becoming a part of it. For many years, the show was my only sanctuary and I still feel a sense of relief every time I step out under the lights.

Touring also gave me an ALL ACCESS pass to my favourite anesthetics, alcohol and cannabis, and I spent the better part of my life on the road comfortably numb. The bus was a well-insulated bubble complete with "best friends" and a fully stocked open bar. On the road we lived in a state of perpetual adolescence, where our problems could always be deferred. I had a reputation for being a big partier but in reality I was always too anxious to visit the local bars after our shows, preferring instead to curl up in the back lounge with a bottle of single malt whiskey and a great big joint.

Sweet oblivion.

Problem was, I could stay up all night doing just that, and more often than not, I did. When the rest of the boys came back from the pub I'd still be there, bombed out of my mind in the back lounge and all good to keep going until daylight. I was the nightcap that never ended and they slowly learned to sneak back into their bunks without engaging me if they wanted to enjoy any quality of life the next day. Those who chose to brave the back-lounge door after last call were doomed to suffer an incapacitating hang-over the next day. This unfortunate condition was disrespectfully known as "getting McCann'd" and it eventually followed me home, where my local friends would often suffer the same fate after being trapped for hours in the Bucket of Blood. When it came to drinking, I had no "off" button. When I picked up a bottle, I was incapable of putting it back down again until it was empty. People around me learned that before they sat down to drink with me, they should be prepared to take the next day off.

This is the person I was when I first met Andrea, and for a time she was almost able to keep up with me, but becoming a mom put an abrupt end to the late-night aspects of our relationship. Pregnancy demands sobri-ety, a language foreign to me, then and, in retrospect, I was completely unprepared for my new parental reality. Raising a baby with an alcoholic who lived in a house with its own fully stocked basement bar was quickly becoming unbearable for Andrea, so when she became pregnant with our second son, Finnegan, the decision was made to move away from the hyper-social downtown core and into the relatively quiet domesticity of the suburbs. My beloved Bucket of Blood booze-basement was traded in for a great big backyard.

I was sad to leave my excellent liquor haven behind, but I agreed, at least on a rational level, given the new status of our quickly growing family, that these were sensible and necessary changes. Keegan was walking and soon would need a place to run, and dungeon bars painted blood red are no place for a playpen. But addiction is not rational. It doesn't care if you have a child to look after or a wife to love. Addiction is an unrelenting hunger that wants to eat you alive, and it will hunt you down wherever you hide. No place is safe. Not even a suburban cul-de-sac. Our life may have moved uptown, but my habit just moved from the darkness of a smoky basement to a brightly lit Corian-coated kitchen.

The constant demands of being a daddy kept me sober during my days at home—at least while Keegan was awake—but I found myself counting the minutes until bedtime and my instant liquid relief. Andrea and I would often gather at the kitchen counter, exhausted after a long day of parenting, and crack open a bottle of wine to take the edge off. This ritual seemed to work for a short time, but soon my habitual cravings began to demand more. Second bottles were cracked and most of those I drank alone. Hangovers didn't really bother me. After thirty years of heavy drinking, my tolerance was high and I was generally able to function fairly well on these relatively low doses. This was not the extreme intake I enjoyed while on the tour bus but it was constant and deliberate alcohol consumption and it began to affect our marriage. Andrea had no real idea how much I was drinking every night when I was away, but she knew I was using too much now at home. I think she also began to realize around this time how serious my problem had become. I may have been married to her, but I was in love with the bottle and our relationship started to unravel as I slowly lost control.

During this time, the band became less active as members pursued solo endeavours and I found myself at home more than ever before. One might think this a positive development for a new father like me—a chance to spend more time with my young family—but I wasn't a typical father. I was a raging alcoholic rock star dad and these extensive hiatuses were keeping me from my fix. I tried to keep myself busy writing and recording songs and even released a couple of distinctly un-sober solo albums: *Lullabies For Bloodshot Eyes* in 2010 and *Son Of A Sailor* in 2011.

Lullabies was dedicated to Keegan and Finn and was intended as an affirmation of how having children can fundamentally change your life. Bookended by actual lullabies I'd written, the album is actually a desperate cry for help from a man who can see the trouble he's sinking into but feels incapable of avoiding. When I listen to it now, I hear the helplessness in my voice and remember how much pain I was in when I wrote those songs.

How much pain we were in.

The Great Big Studio on Water Street had become my new back-lounge drinking bubble. Pressure mounted as my local nights in the shop got progressively later and the rivets of my relationship with Andrea began to pop. I remember waking up on the garage floor one night because I'd been too loaded to fit my key into the front door. Another night I was dropped off on our front step incoherent after collapsing in the bathroom of a downtown dive bar. On my fortieth birthday, I woke up face down on a friend's kitchen floor with a cracked tooth and nasty road rash on my face. I had no idea how I got there. My old habit was beginning to resent the restrictions imposed by domestic life. The beast was getting restless and wanted out of its cage.

Our once-happy marriage was now a war zone and the risk of civilian casualties was high. Every day felt riddled with friendly fire as we tried to co-parent while avoiding eye contact and the ever-growing elephant in the room. I loved my wife and I loved my kids but I remember feeling like I was doomed to lose them; like our fate was predetermined and there was nothing I could do to change it. I was convinced it was only a matter of time before I did something completely unforgivable and Andrea left me. I felt like a passerby pulling over to stare at the still-flaming car wreck that was my life.

The secret I had yet to confront was killing me slowly from the inside like a cancer, lethal and invisible. Truth could be my only chemotherapy but I remained unwilling to accept its painful side effects. So I strapped on my seat belt and waited for the windshield to shatter.

Razor and Rust

What makes you think you're so tough
Forgive me if I call your bluff
Bones and knives, sticks and stones
With every weapon, I have grown

We are razor, we are rust
We are ashes and dust to dust
I'm not ready to give up tonight

I'll ask no mercy, show no fear
You can lock me up for 100 years
Sling your arrows, let them fly
I won't beg, no I won't cry

We are razor, we are rust
We are ashes and dust to dust
I'm not ready to give up tonight

There will be no second chance
The time has come, mount your best defense
There's no need for us to let it slide
No how or when or who or why

We are razor, we are rust
We are ashes and dust to dust
I'm not ready to give up tonight

DOING FINE

THE UNFORTUNATE THING about denial is that you don't realize you are in it until it's way too late and everything is already falling apart. For twenty-five years I had successfully hidden in plain sight and used copious amounts of booze to hold my secret in and my pain at bay. As I entered my forties, my frequent binges were often punctuated by blackouts; more often than not, I'd wake up with no memory of how the previous night had ended. I began to suspect what most people around me had known for years: I might have a drinking problem.

One horribly hungover morning, after repeated apologies, I did what I have since learned many addicts often do. I went online and googled the term "alcoholic." I found a wealth of information and questionnaires and I passed all of them with flying colours. I wasn't surprised. Deep down I had known for a long time what I was. I just didn't want to admit it. If anything, I was slightly relieved by my self-diagnosis because even when I was at my worst in terms of consumption, I always remained a high-functioning logistical problem solver and was accustomed to achieving success, at least in business. Now that I knew for sure what my problem was, I would just do what I always did and solve the problem. The solution was obvious and simple: I would quit drinking.

No problem.

I think my first attempt lasted about three weeks; my second, less than three days. I kept trying but seemed incapable of resisting the many temptations to drink that cornered me in every aspect my life. For the first time in my forty-five years, I experienced real failure. This left me feeling depressed and hopeless, which made me want to drink even more. I had a wife and two young children at home and I knew that with every drink I was letting them down.

But I still drank.

My depression slipped slowly into despair and I could feel myself, one day at a time, giving up on the rest of the life that lay before me. I understand now why so many addictions end in death. It is a chronic disease that slowly wears its victims down so far and brings them so low they can never get back up. Addiction is a parasite that holds its host as near to death as possible for as long as it can without actually killing it.

It is a battle that spares no prisoners.

A war of attrition.

An open wound.

❧

SON OF A SAILOR was released in January 2011. My several attempts at sobriety had failed and my relationship with Andrea was at an all-time low. The band was enduring another self-imposed hiatus, but I was determined to get out of the house, so I hastily hired a backup band and hit the road.

The tour was an unmitigated disaster. Poorly managed and completely under-promoted, we found ourselves performing to half-empty houses (if we were lucky) across the eastern seaboard of the United States, and my dreams of solo stardom were torn slowly from my heavily bleeding heart. The entire tour was a failure and whatever was left of my already low self-esteem was completely destroyed.

So I drank.

A lot.

Only this time I didn't have my back-lounge tour-bus bubble to hide away in. This time I was unravelling out in the open, fully exposed for everyone to see. They say an alcoholic needs to hit rock bottom before he can turn himself around; I'd just taken a swan dive into the deep end of an empty pool and was about to come face-to-face with mine.

The bingeing and blackouts continued throughout that ill-fated tour until I finally found my own rock bottom in a Buffalo, New York, bar. I drank way too much and put myself in harm's way with a Great Big Sea fanatic who was waiting in the wings and ready to pounce. I have no memory of the actual incident (a greater mercy than I deserve), but I remember waking up naked on the floor of my hotel room wondering how I got there... and with whom. I had lost control and put the family I loved in peril. I was terrified Andrea would find out and take the kids and leave me all alone. I have never before felt so ashamed of myself and I tried to bury this secret deep down alongside the dark pain I'd been carrying around for three decades, but this time it was more than I could bear. After a few days back home, racked with guilt and broken by despair, I knew I would have to come clean.

Doing Fine

I get up every morning
Make my empty bed
Feathers in my pillow
Feel like bullets in my head
I start to remember all the wicked words I said
And wonder why I'm lying here alone

Put some water in the kettle
Try and find the phone
To call someone who'll listen
But there's no one that I know
I wonder who was out last night?
Who paid to see the show
And where else I'm not allowed to go

Just when I thought it couldn't get any worse
Somebody put me under some kind of curse
I feel like I drank a full barrel of wine
Man I feel like this most of the time
But other than that, I'm doing fine

The hair of a dog, it hasn't bit me yet
But I can't remember what I'm trying to forget
On women, wine, and whiskey
I'm laying down my bets
But blood flows slowly from a stone
Somebody put me under
Somebody put me down
My head is pounding thunder
And my heart can't take it
No...

I get up every morning
Make my empty bed
Feathers in my pillow
Feel like bricks on my head

Just when I thought it couldn't get any worse
Somebody put me under some kind of curse
I feel like I drank a full barrel of wine
Man I feel like this most of the time
But other than that, I'm doing fine

INTO BLACK

♡

THE EVENING OF November 9, 2011, started out like any other. Séan and I were doing the nightly routine with the kids of bath, jammies, and then shortly thereafter, bed. For us, that meant it was almost time for wine-o-clock, our own nightly routine, which involved opening at least one bottle of wine, possibly two, before retiring to our rooms...separate rooms. Séan had started regularly sleeping in the guest room because he "needed sleep," and, well, with two small kids, uninterrupted sleep in the night is as rare as a unicorn, so instead of being bothered by us, he chose to ignore us and sleep elsewhere.

At least that's what I told myself.

Things had continued to disintegrate with our relationship. Keegan was six and Finn was three-and-a-half so we were busy to say the least. Séan had recently released his second solo album, *Son of a Sailor*, and spent the late summer and early fall touring it. Solo. His first solo tour ever. On top of that, we had play dates for the kids, exercise to try and squeeze in, dogs to walk, kids to walk, touring, songwriting for GBS records, GBS obligations, and on and on. In essence, there was time for everything else on the schedule but us. Séan and I had perpetuated and perfected our roommate status going on six years now.

As with many households, Séan and I had our own domestic responsibilities. We would work through the day and night to get those "chores" done and meet up at the end of the night for our congratulatory bottle, toasting ourselves for how awesome we were doing, then promptly go to our separate rooms. Our marriage was clearly in crisis, the slow meandering kind that seeps into your bones quietly, like a cancer, so you don't even know it's happening. One day you look up and you're not even sleeping in the same bed anymore, and somehow that's the new normal. It was the type of quiet, consistent crisis where you feel your intimacy slipping away but you don't even really fight for it anymore because, let's be honest, you're too damn tired. And you don't feel that pretty, anyway, so why even bother? And forget about having an orgasm, because your entire essence is so wrapped up in being a mommy that those selfish pleasures barely even matter.

Our marriage was a house that was burning one room at a time, until that night when the entire fucking thing exploded and I was left on my knees in the ashes.

That night, when the kids were finally asleep, I went down to our kitchen where I knew Séan would be waiting with the bottle of wine we had opened before putting the babies to bed. Opening a bottle of wine pre-bedtime usually meant it was going to be a two-bottle night. Fine with me. Shit had been more strained than normal in our roommate dance lately. Ever since getting back from the second leg of this solo tour, Séan had been more distant than usual. His "re-entry" period had set a more sombre mood in the house than was typical.

A re-entry period for us was about a two- to three-day day period after tour where Séan had to get used to not being on the road and or performing every night. A time where he had to try to assimilate back into our familial fold and become Séan the Dad, and let go of Séan the Rock Star. It had to be hard on the ego. He wasn't adored (in the same way) every night, people weren't clapping for him for simply existing, and he definitely was not getting any pats on the back. No, at home he had expectations placed on him every minute of every day not only by the two small humans who adore him, but also by me, who, by the time he was home from tour, needed to be away from those two small humans for a while. So those first two or three days back from tour were tricky. I had learned that I had to ease him back into the family life. I had also learned that a great motivator to assist in the transfer of duties was sex. As lacking as our sex life was at that point, I could definitely count on Séan being more than happy to have sex when he got home from tour, and if I had to use that "tool" to bring him back around to family life, I'd take one for the team. But ever since getting back from this tour, sex hadn't been on the table. I'd broached it a couple times only for him to tell me he was too tired or he had something to do or whatever else he came up with. It was very confusing to me. He would barely kiss me this time. He definitely wasn't touching me with any sort of intimacy and he was just generally not present with me. Little did I know that his distance reflected far more than his inability to readjust to life at home.

I sat at the kitchen island, poured myself a glass of the open wine, took a big gulp, and looked at him. Something was up. Being the peacemaker I am, the role I've become so adept at playing since my teenage years and had honed with Séan's increasingly foul moods, I tried to make the situation lighter and say, "Are you going to leave me or something? Seriously, what's going on with you?" I laughed at the absurdity of the thought I'd just put out into the open. Yet, there he stood, hands on the counter, head bowed between his shoulders, not looking at me.

Oh shit, I think to myself.

And then, unable to look me in the eye, he says, "I have something to tell you."

Fuck. I drink another huge gulp of wine. "What did you do?" I seethe.

"I think I slept with someone and I think I may have caught something from her."

I can't believe my ears. I whisper-shout, "What the fuck are you talking about?! You THINK you caught something from her? You THINK you slept with her? Who? What happened? WHAT THE FUCK DID YOU DO, SÉAN?!"

I am shaking, unable to control my physical reaction to this news. At the same time I am unbelievably calm because I guess I knew. I knew that it was only a matter of time before he did this, considering the downward spiral we'd been on.

Séan explained that he didn't remember any of the night in question, but that the woman had reminded him a few weeks later at one of his shows, and he panicked.

As he pieced the memories together for me, I couldn't help but recall this person in my mind's eye. I knew her. I thought I knew her. She'd been a regular GBS fan since I'd been around. She mainly stayed in the background but the crew knew her well, as she was always buying bottles of booze for the band whenever she met up with them.

I had even INVITED her to dinner with us one night after his solo performance in Halifax. In no way did I see this person as a threat. I had even talked to her about Séan's excessive drinking that night—a few measly months before this incident. Little did I know she was a wolf in sheep's clothing, waiting for her opportunity.

On my insistence, he called her. I remember the conversation almost verbatim because I made Séan put her on speaker. When asked, she casually mentioned what she had attempted to do before quickly discovering Séan was too drunk to do much of anything. She mentioned how very, very drunk he was. That he had been slurring.

He hung up and looked almost expectantly at me and I didn't disappoint: "YOU'RE. A. FUCKING. ASSHOLE!!!!!!!! YOU JUST RUINED OUR FAMILY!!!!!!"

I had finished the first bottle of wine and opened a second. I got up from the counter. *Don't cry. Don't cry. Whatever you do, don't let him see you fucking cry!* I thought to myself as he came around the counter towards me.

"I know, I'm so sorry. I'm so sorry. I won't drink again. I promise. I just don't remember anything. I must have completely blacked out because I don't remember anything. I'm sorry. I'm just so sorry."

I grabbed my bottle of wine and turned away to go upstairs, "FUCK! YOU!" I said as a parting shot. I went upstairs, shut the door to my room because my babies were sleeping and I would not let them see me like this, and I disintegrated into an emotional abyss.

I was a mess. I cried constantly for three days, although not in front of my kids. I knew I was quickly falling apart and that I needed space to think. The charred remains of our house and relationship burned me every time I walked through it. I needed to get away. I remember thinking, *How did I ever let it get this bad?* I'd had almost six years' warning leading up to this event and I'd kept my head buried in the sand the entire time. Thinking back to my mother and her situation way back when, the comparisons were undeniable. To me, that was tragic.

I left for Montreal, by myself, four days after that fateful night. Montreal, a city where Séan and I had made beautiful, romantic memories in the infancy of our relationship. I gave myself three days to find clarity and make a decision: was I going to leave or was I going to stay and fight? I had always told myself (and Séan) that cheating was my line in the sand. Since I had committed to not cheating in this relationship (a promise I kept), I expected the same of him, and if he didn't or couldn't do it, I'd walk away. I'd even had it written into our cohabitation agreement that if he cheated on me, he had to admit it to our friends and family before I would leave. So I left to find some peace and insight.

When I was in Montreal I had several over-the-phone sessions with a therapist my sister recommended to me. It was the first therapy I'd gone through since my teen years. Clearly, I needed it. Dr. Jan helped me begin to realize a couple of things. One, I'd been a complicit enabler of Séan's drinking for pretty much the entirety of our relationship. It was fine when it worked for me, and when it didn't work for me it wasn't, but in both cases I was a willing participant in his drinking, having my reasons for both. I could drink with him when I wanted, and keep him on the outside when I wasn't drinking. Both options allowed me to not deal with the demise of our marriage. Two, I had been putting off dealing with the ramifications of his drinking and our shitty relationship to the detriment of all of us: me, Séan, and our family. And three, I had a choice to make. Was this relationship something I wanted, and if it was, was I willing to work my ass off for it? As my therapist warned me, it was going to be a gruelling uphill battle, and it very well could end anyway. I guess what she was trying to tell me was that it was time to shit or get off the pot.

I've never been a person who believes parents or partners should stay together for the sake of their children. I had seen my own parents stay together for far too long and my experience had taught me that when parents have a bad relationship, children suffer. Kids are acutely aware of the stress and tension carried by their parents. They internalize what they see. I strongly believe that a continued disconnect between parents only shows a child what behaviours they can or should accept from their future partners. If what they're living through and being shown is anger, stress, fighting, and the opposite of love, how are they expected to know that they should actually expect more? I certainly didn't believe this to be the case for Séan and me. I knew that if I left he would still be the boys' dad, but I was not going to stay for them. I refused to continue the legacy for them started by my own parents. But, and this is the rub for me, I knew that the man I loved—and I did still love him even if I didn't like him very much at that moment—was a way better human being than even he knew. I believed in Séan, even after all we had been through. Also, as you may have noticed by now, I am always up for a challenge. I decided I would walk away from us by my own decision, not because some fucking disease wanted to take my family from me. Nope. I was all-in and ready for the fight.

I left Montreal determined. I wasn't willing to let Séan, his drinking, or me sabotage us. I was still desperately in love with this man, and a life without him wasn't even within my frame of reality. He was my life. We had a symbiotic relationship and absolutely needed each other to thrive in this world; I knew that in my bones. It was interesting that up until this point neither of us had used the term "alcoholic." We had not confronted this big fucking elephant in our relationship. After Montreal, that beast had a name and we were going to say it until the word held no meaning; we were going to beat that beast into submission.

When I came back home I gave Séan the ultimatum: either stop drinking or I was taking the kids and moving to Minnesota. It was the first and only time I spoke those words. I also told him I wanted to try to make us work again, but I needed time. Time and proof he actually wasn't going to drink again. We had been living as roommates for so long, and continuing that path was easy enough as I sorted through my feelings of betrayal and hurt. Conscious or not, his cheating on me had brought up a lot of unresolved insecurities I had been carrying around. It seemed we both had quite a bit of work to do to get ourselves, and our relationship, back on the right path.

When he pushed his glass of wine away that night after confessing to me, it would be his last.

❧

I KNOW NOVEMBER 9, 2011, is the day Séan celebrates his sobriety. I know that should make me happy. I know it's a big marker in his life because it represents the day he chose me and our family over his addiction.

While all of that is true, I still can't bring myself to celebrate that day. It shouldn't have had to happen that way; however, I don't know if he'd be sober now if it hadn't. While he now considers that day his new birthday, it was truly the day so much of me died.

ONE GOOD REASON

ON NOVEMBER 9, 2011, I told Andrea the truth about what had happened even though I knew it would hurt her deeply and could mean the end of our marriage. She was destroyed, and I was certain that we were, too, but instead of taking the boys and walking out the door she gave me one last chance.

She was clear as a bell and I knew she really meant what she said. I'd been nursing a glass of California chardonnay before our conversation. I laid it down on the kitchen counter and quietly walked away. I haven't touched a drop since. And I never will.

Andrea died a little bit that day. I will never truly know the full extent of the pain I caused, but her incredible loyalty gave me the one good reason I needed to keep going. She single-handedly saved my life with her love, and I vowed to never let her down that way again.

One Good Reason

I never saw it coming
It happened so fast
Hit me like a headstone
Over broken glass
Water is rising
Hard to breathe
Just one good reason
Is all I need
Look out the window
I touch the pane
Every raindrop
Calls out your name
See the clouds rolling
Across the sky
Feel like I'm broken
But I don't know why

You
Were so hard to hold onto
With every tear I cry
I start to realize
I'll never get over you

I remember every minute
I remember the day
When you had to admit it
And our world blew away
That sinking feeling
Down on my knees
A heart revealing
A home in need

Stop looking over your shoulder
For something you won't find
I guess we gotta get over ourselves
Sometimes

So tell me a story
Throw me a line
I'm tired of keeping track of your lives
Feel like I'm falling
Into black
Give me one good reason
And I'll come back

You
Were so hard to hold onto
With every tear I cry
I start to realize
I'll never get over you

STRONGER

STAYING SOBER IS no easy task for any addict, but it's especially difficult when you sing in the biggest party band in Canada. My daily life was fraught with temptation and constant opportunities to drink. Alcohol was a very big part of our carefully constructed "brand" and drinking was something I often felt I was expected to do. Great Big Sea had always been very careful to align itself with the provincial department of tourism's marketing propaganda and a big part of their agenda was to seduce mainlanders to come visit the never-ending party that was now the Newfoundland brand. This was a relationship forged in nods and winks and old black rums. It was our part to play the lovable rogues and lucky bastards who sailed across the sea to entertain the Canadian masses with song and drink and perpetuate the notion that in Newfoundland it would never be too late to hear last call. It was a simple concept and required us to say little and drink lots, which totally worked for my whiskey-sodden old self. The formula made us a lot of money, but if I had the chance to do it all again, I would definitely say a lot more and drink a lot less.

The longest stretch I could ever remember being sober since high school was for two weeks when I caught a really bad flu. Now, I was walking on eggshells trying not to crack because I knew what the consequence would be. Andrea was supportive but she was also very hurt and we really didn't know if we could rebuild our relationship. All we knew for sure was that the drinking would have to stop forever if there was any chance of our marriage surviving.

I had been drinking heavily for almost thirty-five years, so my withdrawal was intense. After three months dry, I began to have nightmares about the priest and what he had done to me. I would wake up in the middle of the night in a cold sweat, screaming, trying to fight off his attacks, but my arms and legs were paralyzed. I felt like I was suffocating in a deep, dark hole. Buried alive. Flashes of my lost teenage innocence haunted me like vengeful ghosts. Pain long buried slowly resurfaced; a phantom limb tingling, trying to wake up and bleed. I needed my anesthetic.

Alcoholics drink for a reason, and I was slowly dying of thirst.

One day I got so desperate I went out and bought a bottle of Lagavulin whisky. I set it on the kitchen table and desperately longed to reach over and open it and let the warm liquid melt the trouble from my mind. I stared at that bottle for a very long time, and as the seconds slowly passed I began to see another object take shape in my peripheral vision, something warm and familiar. It was my guitar, Old Brown, hanging on the wall some twenty feet away. As he came into focus, I realized that I had an option. I left the whiskey on the table and picked up my old guitar instead.

Old Brown is a 1989 Takamine EN-10 guitar I purchased for eight hundred dollars in St. John's when I was twenty-two years old. At the time I didn't know a single chord, but I was determined to learn how to play it and now I know all three chords. For twenty-eight years, he has been my constant companion and has literally held me up for many a pub anthem in hundreds of filled-to-capacity frozen Canadian hockey rinks. When everyone else in my world disappeared and I was left all alone to face my Truth, Old Brown was there for me.

I poured my heart into my guitar and a different kind of song began to emerge. These weren't songs about drinking my problems away, but songs that enabled me to face my truth head-on and free myself from a secret that was slowly killing me.

"Stronger" is the first song I wrote as a sober person. I was forty-four years old. After almost thirty years of shame, I finally began to feel that I might actually be worth fighting for.

Stronger

Been a long time now
Since you left me here alone
But I don't mind 'coz I have grown
I feel all right, something must be wrong
Gonna take my time to sing my song
I am stronger

It was one big lie
Now I can't believe my eyes
But I'm not the kind to lay down and die
You can fool me once, that's on me
But try it twice and you will see

I am stronger, better every day
Stronger, and I got something to say
Stronger, deeper than the sea
Stronger than I ever used to be

When it all comes down
You'll be nowhere to be found
But I'll be standing here
I'll still be around
I'll take this old guitar
And fill it with my heart
I'll show the world I'm ready
To make a brand new start

For I am stronger than all your sticks and stones
Stronger, I know where I am going
Stronger, brighter than the sun
Stronger, and I've only just begun

If it takes a thousand years
For the truth to break
I will overcome my fears
And set the record straight
For I am stronger

help your self

PART IV

EXODUS

SOBER SIDE EFFECTS

♡

I DON'T KNOW what I expected with a sober Séan. I think I thought if he just stopped drinking everything with us would go back to normal; I wasn't even thinking about the "why" part of his drinking. What I quickly realized, however, was that we really didn't have a "normal." What had started out as fun when we first met had become habitual and necessary for us to maintain communication. Séan and I drinking, or just Séan drinking, was how we communicated. Clearly this was neither healthy nor normal.

Eight days after Séan quit drinking we had a social event to attend at Keegan's school. It was the school's annual fundraiser and Séan and Alan were performing a short set for entertainment, so we had to go. This was two days after I'd returned from Montreal. Wounds were fresh. Sobriety was fresher. Before their set, Alan went up to the bar and returned with a couple drinks. One for him and one for Séan. He put a whiskey in front of Séan, thinking, I believe, his quietness was due to nerves. This was a person who'd been touring and singing with Séan for the entirety of his adult life; he knew what he thought were the signs of nerves, as Séan always had a bit of stage fright. Without a word to either of them, I grabbed the whiskey and drank it down in one gulp. Five minutes later I noticed another drink in front of Séan. Again, I drank it myself. When I saw Alan going up to get another round I turned to him and said, "Séan's not drinking" and turned back around, ignoring whatever fallout I may have caused. So began our journey into a sober life.

By the time Séan got sober, the dynamics in Great Big Sea had changed drastically and all three members were doing solo projects. Alan was chasing movie stardom and brighter lights, Bob was writing and seemingly trying to find a place to land in the middle between Alan, who wanted to do different, non-GBS things, and Séan, who wanted the band to work, i.e. bring in money. I believe Séan just wanted to keep the band moving forward, making money and keeping busy, while somehow remaining sober. At least that's the way it looked from my perspective.

Moreover, as Séan's social circle started to change, so too did mine. My friendships with people in and around the band started to deteriorate—in no small part because I was done listening to people use Séan as the poster boy for bad behaviour. I knew that characterization had suited him while he was drinking. I knew he had behaved poorly in and around the band at times, but I couldn't accept that label being thrust on him as we were fighting for his sobriety. It seemed to me that many people preferred a drunk (unconscious) Séan to the alert, highly caffeinated, energized version he was becoming. The people I had surrounded myself with preferred the status quo, and I wasn't willing to accept their preconceived and unchanging version of my husband. This is an issue I've heard many recovering addicts echo. It seems my "friends" were no different, and as much as everything was changing for Séan and me, they seemed more comfortable with everything staying the same. I found after I told some close friends about the troubles we had gone through with the cheating, and explained why Séan wasn't drinking anymore, these friendships fractured even more.

I fully blame myself. I was the one who changed the rules.

Séan's eyes were clear and sober for the first time since I'd met him and I saw him trying to keep his business viable and creative in the face of divided shareholder attention spans. I, however, couldn't stand the hypocrisy I was seeing in how people within the GBS orbit expected everything to be the same, both work-wise and socially. I felt like a fraud every time we all sat down at an overpriced St. John's restaurant for the sake of keeping up band appearances. I couldn't be blindly supportive of actions and decisions other band members were making that were directly affecting Séan's livelihood and my family's financial well-being. I wouldn't put my head in the sand again, and I couldn't pretend there wasn't another elephant in the room. Séan had constantly been painted as the villain in that trio. He was often labelled the "moody one" or the "angry one" and, at times, the "drunk one." Certainly, there were times in the past when his drinking had adversely affected his bandmates. Séan knew that and, as a sober person, was trying to do better and be a better partner. Yet, it seemed pretty apparent that his efforts were both unsupported and unwanted. The strain and divisiveness I was feeling in my personal relationships were being mirrored in what I saw happening to Séan in his work life. I couldn't do fake anymore. And I figured these people didn't want to do fake anymore either, so I cut ties and didn't look back.

(That's a lie. I totally looked back all the time, but I was now just as much an outsider as Séan, and there was no going back.)

Séan and I were trying to find our new reality. He was still very moody and seemed quite depressed. I chalked that up to detox the first few months, but it persisted. And though we fought, and though I still had to work through my hurt about the cheating, we didn't give up on each other.

The year 2012 was one of not much work on the road for Séan, as he was busy pulling together archival materials for GBS's twentieth-anniversary album, and that kept him as occupied as possible until the record was released. This was both good and bad for us because I had come to the conclusion long ago that Séan and I work because he goes away. It works for both of us. We love each other, but we need breaks from each other. I will never be embarrassed about that. Little did I know at the time this lighter GBS touring schedule was a sign of things to come, and we would eventually, once again, have to find our new normal.

In February 2012 we went on a two-week family vacation with non-band friends...and a three-months'-sober Séan. It was mostly fine, but Séan was still pretty surly most of the time. I had told him before we left that if he didn't want me drinking around him, or even at all, I wouldn't, but he insisted it would be fine. To this day, he knows that's my standing dictum and there have been times when he's told me he's on shaky ground. Drinking is no longer my thing. Yes, I love a great glass of wine, especially after being with the kids ALL THE TIME, but I don't need it. And I certainly won't sacrifice his health or our family for it. I still wasn't sure if this new sobriety was going to stick, but I was hopeful and willing to take his brooding and bad moods. At least now when he was angry he wasn't drunk, too. Silver lining?

The first big test of Séan's sobriety was Great Big Sea's tour in Australia. I knew the twenty-five-plus-hour flight was going to take its toll on someone who was used to getting drunk twice on the way to Vancouver. I'd be lying if I said I wasn't worried. Petrified, actually. It was March 2012, just four months into Séan's sober life, and I knew he was having some difficulties, though he wasn't necessarily talking to me about them. His mood had taken a particularly dark turn and I was worried that whatever was eating him alive was going to cause him to break on that flight. I sent him off with the best armour I could muster, our love and my belief in him. I packed this in his laptop case for him to find on the plane.

> I love you.
>
> I believe in you.
>
> You are strong enough to do this flight booze free ...stronger than everyone else we know.
>
> We will miss you dearly.
>
> I hope Australia is AMAZING. ...please try to find something amazing every day to tell us about.
>
> Open yourself up like a spring flower to everything this trip wants to give you.
>
> Breathe.
> Live.
> ...xoxo... Smile...
> I love you — I believe in you. A.

He made it through the awful plane ride round trip as well as the tour of Australia, and I was SO proud of him. Little victories were cause for celebration in our house. Meanwhile, the boys and I surrounded ourselves with a new group of friends that didn't come with the GBS history.

Finding new friends wasn't so hard for the boys; they were both young and just starting to find playmates in their respective schools, but it was a bit hard for me, putting myself back out there at the age of forty-one. Small price to pay, really. However, surrounding myself with people who loved my kids, me, and my sober husband, no matter how crabby he was, quite possibly saved my marriage. I often talk about this group of people as my "tribe." I believe every mom needs a tribe. It can be small, it can be big, but being without a tribe, a.k.a. a group of moms you can depend on, cry with, rejoice with, and generally bitch to, can lead you down a path of isolation. Feeling alone and believing you're alone when you're walking the motherhood path and the addictions recovery path is a recipe for failure in my opinion. Maybe I'm just not strong enough to do it on my own, but my tribe was my "partner" when my partner went insular and couldn't, or wouldn't, let me in.

Séan and I still existed as roommates for a good part of 2012. We kept fighting for us, but we were finding out we didn't know who "us" was any-more—maybe we never had. I knew he was struggling with some pretty caustic thoughts running through his head, but he still wasn't talking.

Our battles, I felt, were just beginning.

The Singer Who Lost His Song

A melody lingers in my ear tonight
A lyric ringing loud and clear
Leads me to the light
It's the sound of a young heart breaking
Behind a mind that's wound too tight
Under skin so hot, it's ready to ignite

I turn the radio on and I let the DJ drive
When you're on the road to nowhere
It's hard to stay between the lines
And I see my own star falling
Into the tick and tock of time
Looking for a friend I left behind

And it goes on and on and on...
But you won't know what you're missing
'Til it's gone
It goes on and on and on...
But there ain't nobody listening to
The singer who lost his song

Found a penny in my pocket
And it asked me for some change
The sun came up this morning
So I know it's bound to rain
There's a broken record playing
And I'm haunted by the sound
It keeps my head spinning round and round

A melody lingers in my ear tonight
A lyric ringing loud and clear
Big and strong and bright
It's the sound of an old heart healing
From a wound won in a fight
Because I know this time
I'm gonna get it right
Yes I know this time I'm gonna get it right
Because it goes on and on and on...

THE SINGER WHO
LOST HIS SONG

QUIT SMOKING cigarettes on the same day I quit drinking. I don't really know why. Perhaps I felt guilty for all the harm my addiction had caused—my Catholic genetic code crying out for atonement. Just to make sure I didn't miss out on any suffering, I decided to do this completely cold turkey as well. No nicotine gum, no patch, no hypnosis, and NO MORE Player's Lights. I did it the hard way, and for the record, I do not recommend it. I had tried and failed to quit both before so I was under no illusions that refraining from alcohol and tobacco would be easy, especially at the same time, but I did anticipate some immediate health benefits for my efforts. I was already an athletic singer; a shantyman. I used my voice like a battering ram to blow audiences away at certain key points in the set—to break the monotony and keep the show rolling along. Surely, I thought, in the absence of single malt whiskey and tobacco smoke, my vocal prowess should rise to the scale of Pavarotti.

I was wrong.

Six months after I got clean, I began to experience problems with my voice. I was having trouble hitting high notes and struggled just to make it through the shows. I had kept myself busy writing my new recovery album and my voice needed to be in ship shape by January 2013; that's when I'd be recording with my friend Joel Plaskett what would eventually become the album *Help Your Self*. After consulting some local physicians and speech pathologists I was put on vocal rest for a month, but that only caused my throat to atrophy and made me sound even worse. A real singer's voice is more than just an instrument, it is their identity. Singing was the last coping mechanism I had left and I was losing it fast. After much googling and reaching out to other artists, I eventually found a phenomenal speech and language pathologist: Aaron Low. Trained in circumlaryngeal massage and laryngeal reposturing (in layman's terms, choking), Aaron is an unconventional and cutting-edge healer and his giant hockey player hands worked miracles on my rusty old pipes. The therapy is uncomfortable but extremely effective and I began to see results immediately. In just a few sessions, Aaron was able to pull my voice back into singing shape with his fingers. After our first choking-out session, Aaron intuited that the source of my vocal issues was more mental than physical.

"How are things going with the boys on the bus? Is there currently any stress in the band?"

"It's a band, man. There's ALWAYS stress."

"Understood. But has anything new happened recently? Any major changes made?"

"Well, I did quit drinking about six months ago. I guess that was pretty major...."

"How much did you drink?"

"As much as I possibly could."

"I see," he said slowly while pinching my weezy windpipe between his enormous Moose Jaw farm-boy knuckles. "So you have to quit drinking or you will be kicked out of the band?"

"Nope. The band is very much in favour of drinking. I need to quit drinking or I will be kicked out of my house."

"Oh dear. Are you allowed to drink even a little bit? Like maybe one or two drinks before a show?"

"Unfortunately I am not that kind of drinker...."

"Do you smoke?"

"I did. I gave that up the same day I quit drinking."

"Are you a madman!?"

"By most definitions, absolutely. But what are you getting at? Surely my vocal prowess can only be improved by giving up my bad habits? To be honest, I was expecting to be singing like Freddie Mercury by now...."

"Suddenly refraining from smoke and drink are definitely good things for civilians to do, but for a career singer like you, it can be a huge cause of stress. Your vocal cords are as fine and thin as a butterfly's wings, but over the years you have baked yours hard like boot leather with burning whiskey and boiling hot smoke. Now that you've turned off the furnace, those old leather boots are softening back up into butterfly wings again and they just can't handle the strain."

Let no good deed go unpunished. I may have saved my marriage, but it was about to cost me my career. More than that, my very identity. If I wasn't completely stressed out before I walked into Aaron's office, I certainly was now.

Closer and even more uncomfortable examination with a stroboscopic camera revealed that I had developed a small gelatinous cyst on my right vocal cord. Surgery was an option, but it was not without serious risk and came with no guarantees the offending cyst would not reoccur as soon as I started singing again. Laryngeal massage and an intense vocal warm-up regimen (trill training) might also work but would require substantial effort and time. I decided to opt for the latter first. The surgical alternative would always be there.

I got back on the tour bus armed with an extremely annoying thirty-minute vocal warm-up and a very sore neck. For a time, the mufflerless motorcycle–sounding "trills" (quavering vibratory sounds forced from deep in my diaphragm and out of my mouth) worked very well and, with the exception of some of the really high notes, I felt my old voice slowly return. But sober life on the bus wasn't getting any easier and pressure within the rolling tin can began to build as I struggled to stay dry.

After twenty years spent next to an inebriated "shantyman," I suspect that adjusting to a wide-awake and highly caffeinated McCann was no small adjustment for my bandmates. Whereas before I lived for the most part in blissful ignorance of how this metal ship was run, I was now full of questions and, even worse, suggestions on how I thought we might be able to continue to sustain ourselves financially and artistically as a band. My partners paid some lip service to my new ideas for a time, but eventually stopped listening altogether and waited for me to fall off the wagon and back to sleep like they'd seen me do a hundred times before. We were Canada's favourite party band and the show must go on, regardless of any member's personal recovery commitments. Just because I was making some big life changes didn't mean the bus would follow suit, and that meant I would continue to run into bottles of booze whenever I opened a cooler or a closet or a fridge door. To avoid temptation, I spent more and more time alone in my coffin of a bunk, binge-watching television series and biting my tongue.

GOODBYE, OLD FRIEND

IN 2013 GREAT BIG SEA released a greatest hits box set to celebrate our twentieth anniversary and embarked on the XX Tour. Over the course of 2012 I had tried to keep myself out of trouble by assembling archival materials to include in the box. This afforded me the rare opportunity to relive and reflect on the realities of the past two decades, most of which I'd spent less than completely present. I began to revisit old mistakes and imagine different futures, had better decisions been made.

After several months of sorting through the scattered minutiae of our collective career, I couldn't help but think that somewhere out there on that long, relentless road we had lost our way. Twenty years is a long time for a band to stay together; it's longer than a lot of marriages, and longer than some of us even survive. At forty-five years of age I was trying to sober up from a party that had been going on for decades. I was trying to make some big changes, but the party raged on, so I decided it was time for me to get off the bus for good.

One night while recording *Play* with producer Danny Greenspoon and bitching about some recent touring misfortune, I heard him say something that has always stuck with me: "There's only one thing worse than being in the music business, and that's not being in the music business." Great Big Sea would have to be considered a success by any standard, and my choice to leave was one of the hardest decisions I've ever had to make.

By the end of 2012, I felt we were so far apart on so many levels as a band that it would be best for everyone if I just stepped away, and better for the business if I gave everyone a good head's up. On January 7, 2013,

I tendered my official resignation from the road. Nobody tried to talk me out of it. They just asked me to keep it quiet until the tour was over. So I kept writing songs and got ready to say goodbye.

Despite all predictions to the contrary, I somehow managed to remain sober on the Great Big Bus for the entirety of the XX Tour—a singular accomplishment for which I shall remain forever proud. If I could survive that temptation, I knew I could live through anything without ever drinking again.

The tour was a huge financial success but a disaster on the personal relationship front. If I felt I was being shut out and ignored before, I had now become the invisible man. I was on a bus with ten of my closest friends but I had never felt more isolated and alone. The pressure to drink intensified as the money rolled in and the party on the bus raged on. I had to fight hard every day to stay sober, but I never cracked. I began to duct tape messages of reassurance to myself at the foot of my mic stand every night just to remind myself I was really there.

YES.

GIVE.

FREE.

TRUTH.

GOOD.

TRY. FAIR.

LOVE.

PEACE.

With just two weeks left before the end, and not a single real conversation in months, it became obvious there was no plan to let anyone know that I was really leaving, so I decided to let the truth out myself on November 14, 2013, in a farewell tweet:

> This will be my last tour with GBS...
> and I fully intend to enjoy every fucken second
> and leave the stage with nothing but LOVE in my heart.

I lost three thousand Twitter followers in three hours.

My unilateral announcement went over even less well on the Great Big Bus, where cold indifference turned quickly to vexation. I needed to get off because the stress threatened my sobriety, so Andrea found a sitter and flew up to help me through the last few shows. We rented a car, booked some hotel rooms, and drove to the final gigs on our own. Without her support, I would never have been able to finish the tour.

I really wish I could tell you I left the stage with nothing but love in my heart but that would be untrue. I tried very hard but I walked away feeling hurt and humiliated and betrayed—feelings I remembered well from a wound sustained a long time ago.

And still feel today.

❦

WALKING AWAY FROM Great Big Sea is one of the hardest things I have ever had to do, but I have learned that just because a thing is difficult doesn't mean it isn't the right thing to do. In my experience, I have actually found the opposite to be true. It is often the arduous path that leads us to the most rewarding place. The only regret I have is that my former bandmates and I didn't part on better terms.

Our very last show was in Moncton, New Brunswick, on New Year's Eve 2013. It was plastic and perfunctory and only for the money and I really wish now that I hadn't agreed to participate at all. The fans and the band both deserved a better finale.

I always used to complain about walking around St. John's as a Great Big Sea man. The small city-state takes pride of ownership in its homegrown celebrities, and several random and unwanted conversations would have to be suffered before poor old Tosh and Marley could ever see the end of a Bannerman Park walk.

"Are you buddy what plays in the band?"

"I'm one of them."

"Yes b'y! Are you de ugly one or de arsehole?"

The price we pay for fame.

Having said that, I have learned that walking around St. John's as a *former* Great Big Sea man is even worse.

"Are you buddy what quit da band?"

"I had to leave for health reasons."

"What are you—cracked?!"

Membership has its privileges.

There really aren't that many high-paying jobs where I come from, and people had a hard time wrapping their head around whatever my selfish reasons were for departure. In Newfoundland, unlimited access to free booze holds the same spiritual weight as Nirvana, so local support for my decision was not high.

I was the idiot who walked away from a goldmine.

Goodbye Old Friend

I worry about all the time I wasted
Standing in line and putting on faces
Dancing to someone else's tune
Afraid to single someone out
Content to whisper when I should shout
Ignoring the elephant in the room
Always ready to compromise
To make me look good in your eyes
In your hands I was nothing more than clay
But that stops today

Goodbye old friend
I hope we meet again
I'm sure that we'll find something nice to say
Goodbye old friend
Our road's come to an end
And it's time I make my own way

I wondered if I could ever leave you
But then one day I began to see through
All the politics behind your plans
Ever ready for a fight
No matter who was wrong or right
Never even tried to understand
Like a soldier sent to foreign shores
My heart grows weary of this war
I don't think I can face another day
Now all I can say

Goodbye old friend
I hope we meet again
I'm sure that we'll find something nice to say
Goodbye old friend
Our road's come to an end
And it's time I was making my own way

TAKIN' CARE OF BUSINESS

♡

ON JANUARY 7, 2013, Séan told his partners he wanted "out." Specifically, he told them he didn't want to continue as a shareholder anymore, that his equity/shares in the company were up for sale, and that he needed to stop touring to remain sober and physically and mentally healthy. He was finding the stress of the band's wandering priorities too much for his newly sober brain to handle. Let me put it this way: Séan's a 100 percent all-in or all-out guy. He felt that GBS, as a company, wasn't operating at its peak because other projects had started taking priority. Although he himself had produced two solo albums, those projects always took a back seat to what he deemed his first and biggest responsibility, GBS. It was literally his baby that he had worked very hard to create and that was where he intended to forge his legacy. When a baby isn't fed, nurtured, and cared for, it cannot survive. This is what Séan feared was happening, and after three years of infighting he just couldn't take it anymore; he put in his notice and told his business associates he was officially DONE.

But the partners decided not to announce Séan's departure. We all knew this was going to be his last tour with GBS, but it wasn't decided at that January meeting how to make it public. Séan felt they would figure it out as a band as the tour went along. He opted out of doing press and meet-and-greets because, frankly, he didn't know what to say. In his new sobriety he was trying to live as authentic a life as possible, and not telling people what his future plans were, i.e., that he wasn't ever getting on a GBS bus again, wasn't a possibility at that point. Little did either of us know, the plan was to not have a plan, and to not announce Séan's departure.

I remember Séan more than once looking for direction from his partners and management about what to say to the press or to people about his departure and when to say it. His requests were always met with silence. So throughout the tour, Séan continued to say nothing.

Perhaps the biggest disappointment for me as the wife of someone struggling with alcoholism and its demons is seeing which "friends" stick and which ones don't. I never fully understood the relationship dynamic Séan had with his partners. At times it seemed jovial and very friendly and at others it felt cruel and cold. I figured that like any familial relationship, it just ebbed and flowed. Plus, these people had spent more time with each other than most married couples, so there were bound to be latent feelings of unrest and possible ill will. Yet, I always figured they'd have each other's backs if and when the chips were down. I assumed that with a lot of our "friends," but time and time again I was proven wrong. This was one of those times, and it was impossible to hide my disappointment and anger.

I've never thought of myself as a loyal person. Quite the opposite. As a child I was never shown the merits of remaining loyal to anyone. I'd never had a partner I didn't cheat on. I have exactly one friend from my childhood who I'm still friends with. Loyalty wasn't a characteristic I held in esteem. I actually have no idea why this changed with Séan. Love? Desire? All I know is that when I made the decision to move to Newfoundland, Séan and I made a pact that if we wanted out of the relationship we wouldn't cheat, but rather tell the other person and bow out gracefully. A "no harm no foul" type of situation. To this day, we believe we are both allowed to be happy, and if that means without each other, so be it. Maybe this is where my loyalty began. The perceived flagrant violation of loyalty in Séan's business relationships made me very sad—and then very angry. Like most moms I know, you fuck with my family and I will roar like a lion and attack like a bear. I could do nothing about what I was seeing and I hated that all-too-familiar feeling of helplessness. I could only support Séan as best I could while I saw some of the most important relationships of his life wash away.

So basically 2013 started with a couple kicks to the ass of our newly sober lifestyle. First, Séan's announcement to his partners about wanting to sell his shares and stop touring in January, and the silence it was met with, left me pissed and left him pretty hurt. The second was the actual tour itself, which left Séan alone on a bus of ten. I saw my husband grow defeated, sad, tired, and angrier with each new leg of the tour. I was frightened this was going to be the end of his sobriety, and the end of us. I hated that it felt like the fate of my marriage rested on the outside bullshit that was erupting in his work world and that I could do nothing to stop it.

The XX Tour started in March and went the entire year. Séan's last show with GBS was December 31, 2013. I knew he was nervous about getting on the bus. He had survived over a year and a trip to Australia sober, but the challenges that awaited him on the bus and in the dressing rooms played on his mind before he left. I did the best I could to assure him he would be okay, that we would be okay. I was the constant cheerleader to his dreary, worried heart. Honestly, I was worried right along with him. With all the business bullshit going on with his partners, I tried to make our home life as simple and easy as possible. I guess it was my new way of enabling.

We had begun to find our stride as a sober Séan and Andrea with new friends. Our boys were great; Keegan was going on eight and Finn was almost six. Up to this point they had been blissfully unaware of what Séan and I had gone through over the last year and a half, and we kept it that way until slowly, as they aged, we started to tell them our truth. We both thought it was extremely important to be as (age-appropriately) honest with them as possible so they could hear the truth from us and not some slanderous version of it from somewhere else. However, their focus was still mainly inward, not caring much what Mom and Dad did.

What Séan did have, and what did keep him focused, was his work on his new album, *Help Your Self.* He was excited to get into the studio with Joel Plaskett. It was an excitement I hadn't seen in him since before we'd had kids. Just that little glimmer of a happy, unburdened Séan gave me great hope. I carried the memory of it with me for a long time.

Séan left for the first leg of the XX Tour at the beginning of March 2013 and would be gone for three weeks. Until now, the two-week Australia tour in 2012 had been his longest period of sobriety while on the road. This trip was a week longer and on the bus, which always included lots of downtime.

So I loaded him up with every talisman I had and assured him he would be all right. I was worried enough for the both of us but in no way would I show him. I made arrangements to be with him as much as I could for these last GBS shows even though I knew I would (and ultimately did) run into the woman who had tried to fuck my husband when he was blackout drunk.

Let's be clear: Séan was blacked out when he (tried) to cheat with her. Worse, she knew his proclivities after being around him so much at his shows. If the situation were reversed, and Séan took home a girl who was blackout drunk, what would we call it?

Fate did not disappoint.

Having done my homework on the enemy-at-hand, I knew the most likely place to run into her was Chicago, her hometown. But I was with my sister and we were taking shots like they were water, so I was itching for the fight I got. Through our taunting and my sister's eventual warning to this woman to "Stay the fuck away from my family," this woman and I had our very public, very loud confrontation after the show. I said some horrible words to this person and showed all of my worst insecurities and hurt to anyone within earshot.

I got tossed right out of the legendary House of Blues. Rightfully so, but I still have no regrets about that scene. I deserved to be heard just as I deserved to be kicked out of the place. Chicago continues to be one of my favourite cities in the world. Maybe, as with most things in my life, I just really like the thing that gives me the biggest challenge.

Séan came home from each leg of the tour just a little more defeated than before. It was honestly all I could do to keep his spirits up and convince him to leave it all on the stage with an open heart. And he wanted to. He wanted the last GBS tour of his life to be fun, light, and carefree. Yet when he saw none of that happening, it started throwing him for a loop. Séan and I were fighting demons on both fronts, but at least for the moment we weren't fighting each other.

In the fall, before the last leg of the tour started, it became pretty apparent the band wasn't going to make an official statement about Séan leaving. Séan and I talked quite a bit about what he should do, and whether or not he should make his own announcement. I told him, as a fan, I would be bummed if I didn't know this was his last tour and found out after the fact. As a fan, maybe I would make an extra effort to go see the band as a whole one last time if I knew this was it.

As he was walking out the door to leave for the airport, he handed me a handwritten note and said, "Don't put this on my Twitter until you know my plane is in the air." Okie dokie. The minute I put it out there, it was the first of two media frenzies I would witness regarding Séan's Twitter.

I'm grateful that during this time Séan had the mixing, mastering, and eventual release of *Help Your Self* to keep him busy and hopeful. Had he not had that to look forward to, I'm not sure he would have made it through being invisible on the bus or having copious amounts of booze passed under his nose daily during that final tour.

Do not misunderstand me, those things that were going on in GBS-world were happening to all of us. Being in that band was a lifestyle, and touring had been Séan's lifestyle for over twenty years. Everything the band did or didn't do affected every part of his life and our life together.

As that life started to wind down, and the impending release of *Help Your Self* was ramping up, it became even clearer to me, through my continued talks with Séan and through these new recordings, that the priest had definitely subjected Séan to more than just emotional abuse.

My initial suspicions began to have legs to stand on the more Séan and I spoke. I don't think I ever asked him straight out, when he was sober, about these suspicions. I knew he would tell me when he could and wanted to, but knowing the devil we were fighting now made my focus laser-sharp.

HELP YOUR SELF

I GOT OFF THE BUS because it was an unhealthy place for a recovering addict, but now I found myself sitting at home looking for something useful to do to keep me out of trouble. I started volunteering at the Janeway Children's Hospital in St. John's, working with music therapists to help patients suffering from both physical and mental illnesses. I got to see the positive effects a song could have on a teenager suffering anorexia and a young girl battling leukemia. Music is strong medicine and I have witnessed it drop the heart rates of kids in the hospital worried about an operation or waiting for their next dose of chemotherapy. I have even seen it bring a smile to a dying boy's face. It's been clinically proven time and again that music helps people feel better without the serious side effects of prescription medication, and I believe that music helped save my life by helping me to face my truth and move forward.

Around that time I also began volunteering with the local chapter of Easter Seals, where I learned how to see the "ability" in "disability" and to always say exactly what I mean. Working with these wonderful human beings really broadened my awareness and boosted my soul. They were friends to me when few were to be found, and I will be forever grateful for the changes they helped me through.

Surviving Great Big Sea was difficult but it was a minor inconvenience compared to the spiritual heavy lifting required for continued sobriety and real personal growth. I was feeling overwhelmed and disoriented and so, once again, I reached out to Old Brown for help. I put my head down and started writing new songs.

Take Off My Armour

I have spent most of my life
Believing that truth was all black and white
But I'm getting tired of this fight
Gonna get off this road
And get on with my life
Gonna let myself go
Gonna let myself wander
Like a river I'll flow
Back to the sea
Gonna let myself go
Take off my armour
Gonna lay down my load
And be free

I'll breathe in, breathe out
Let the wind caress my mouth
Leave behind all fear and doubt
When I breathe in and I breathe out

I have spent most of my life
Singing a song that just wasn't right
Now I see a new end in sight
With a melody strong
And a harmony so bright

Gonna let myself go...

If leaving the band had been treason, then leaving Newfoundland would be nothing short of blasphemy, so I decided to give the island a chance to change my mind before we finally pulled that trigger. I set off for Fogo Island, a wild and beautiful place lashed by wind and water, to clear my mind and let my heart open a little bit wider. According to the Flat Earth Society (and yes, there really is one), Brimstone Head on Fogo Island is one of the four corners of the earth, so, in theory, once you sail past the imposing landmark you run the risk of falling off. I was trying to find my own boundaries, to see how far I was really willing to push myself before I too would fall. In retrospect, my time on Fogo was a test of my own resolve. I spent many hours just looking out my window at the ever-rolling sea, waiting for inspiration, looking for a sign.

As always, it came to me in the form of a song.

The morning I wrote "Take off My Armour," my path became clear. I would find my future by fearlessly walking towards it. It would not be the easy path, but it would prove to be the right one—and I've been following it ever since.

I kept writing songs over the course of 2012 because they helped me feel better and gave me the courage I needed to navigate the treacherous waters of life as a newly sober Great Big Sea man. This was a time of great transition in my life. A rearranging of goals and priorities; an accumulation of courage to capitalize on my second chance. As a family, our lives were radically changing and we had some big decisions to make. All the while, my heart was quietly opening itself up to being fully present—and to all the joy and pain that comes with that.

It was a slow and steady burn.

Songs like "Help Your Self" and "Wish You Well" became my battle cries as I dug in and determined to fight for my sobriety. I felt better every time I sang "Stronger." No matter what mood I happened to be in, it made me smile.

Still does.

Eventually, the new songs began to add up to what I thought might be a full album (remember those?). I have been a longtime fan and have huge respect for Dartmouth, Nova Scotia's number-one son, Joel Plaskett, and when he told me he was coming over to tour "The Rock" with his Emergency band in the fall of 2012, I saw it as a great opportunity to bend his ear and get the record made. Joel is a man of great integrity both musically and as a human being and I trusted him completely with my story. We decamped to his New Scotland Yard studio in January 2013, where I proceeded to let my story unfold over the course of fourteen frozen nights.

Through these songs, I began to tell the world the truth about who Séan McCann really was. This record was extremely personal and raw, and while its creation was very therapeutic for me, I really didn't expect it would mean very much to many others. I also wasn't ready to jump right back out on the road. I had poured my heart into the album, and this time I resolved to do less promotional pitching and let the songs speak for themselves. So instead of using a record label, I quietly released the album, *Help Your Self*, on January 29, digitally. Then I sat back and hoped the good people out there would listen.

Turns out I was wrong. A great many were interested in this new kind of song and I began to receive hundreds of emails and tweets and Facebook messages thanking me for sharing myself so openly and sincerely. These songs were about my own personal struggle with addiction but they had somehow resonated beyond the walls of my own prison. Many people saw themselves or those they loved in my new songs.

"I know that song...that's my mother."

"I know that song...that's my husband."

"I know that song...that song is me."

I had finally shared the truth about my addiction and it had resonated with thousands of people who were just like me. This experience taught me a great lesson: I wasn't alone. It was a huge leap forward and the main reason I am able to remain sober to this day.

☘☙

THE REOPENING OF a broken heart is a delicate and dangerous operation and I was performing the surgery slowly on myself. The initial incision had been coming clean with Andrea on November 9, 2011. Progress had been hindered by layers of scar tissue long hardened over the deep, original cut. Stepping off the Great Big Bus was the sound of my sternum cracking and my chest cavity being pulled back to reveal the injured organ still beating within. Now it was time to clean and re-dress the old and festering wound. The operation would last a lifetime and would be conducted while the patient remained entirely conscious and without anesthetic.

The greatest challenge to overcoming pain is allowing yourself first to actually feel it. I was like a newborn baby again, frightened and small, remembering how to breathe. Andrea was right there watching over me as I began to take my first steps, never letting go of my hand. The hard work of rehabilitation had begun.

I began to document my progress in the form of new songs, and January 2015 found me back in the studio with Joel, recording the lessons I had recently learned. When it was time to lay down the vocal tracks, we both noticed a gentle raspy sound in my voice which we actually liked. The weathered tone felt like a good fit for this thoughtful collection of songs. It was the sound of a weary traveller sharing lessons learned out there on the long, hard road of life. Tired but undefeated. It was the sound of survival.

Early that spring I began to notice the rasp in my voice getting worse, so I flew up to Toronto to visit Aaron at his brand new practice, The Voice Clinic, to see exactly what was going on with my pipes. A thorough stroboscopic examination revealed that the formerly gelatinous cyst on my right vocal cord had hardened and would now have to be surgically removed.

"What happens if I don't have the surgery, Aaron?"

"Your voice will get worse and worse until you can't sing at all."

"And if I go through with it...?"

"Your voice will either be completely restored...or you will never sing again."

Fuck me.

I talked it over with Andrea, and we chose the surgery because it was the only option that included the possibility of me being able to actually sing in the future. Singing had saved my life and neither of us was willing to accept a scenario with a Séan who was unable to do what he was born to do. After thirty years of searching, I was finally beginning to find my true voice and I wasn't about to give it up without a fight.

I went under the knife of a brilliant otolaryngology surgeon, Dr. Manish Shah, on June 16, 2015. Andrea's hand was covering my lips when I came to, to make sure I wouldn't try to speak.

"The operation was a complete success," she whispered. "You will be singing again soon. But you have to give your vocal cords time to heal first. Dr. Shah says you can't say a single word for at least ten days."

She smiled her big beautiful smile and handed me a pen and a notepad. The next ten days would likely be the most peaceful of her life.

The damage to my voice had been brought on by stress. Choosing to live sober and abandoning a life-long career had been incredibly difficult steps to take, both physically and mentally, but I knew they were all necessary to ensure my continued recovery. We did the hard work and we paid a heavy price but we have no regrets because in the end we were successful, and today I can still sing, share, and survive.

❧

I MADE A SUM TOTAL of twelve thousand dollars in 2014. This was a fraction of my former Great Big salary and I began to second-guess myself. Andrea reassured me, but we both began to understand that St. John's was probably not the best place to live if I really wanted my recovery to last. Too much negative history and too much temptation to drink. Add to that living constantly under a microscope, and the mathematical probabilities of success start to tumble like a stagette party on George Street.

It was time for us to move on.

We put our house up for sale in the spring of 2015 and started looking in Minneapolis, Minnesota, and Ottawa, Ontario, for a new home. Andrea is from Minneapolis and still has family there, so that potential move made sense. We found some good options and even went as far as to bid on one house, but something always kept us from closing the deal in America. Ottawa is very much like Minneapolis in many ways. It is peppered with lakes and farms and its people are very warm and friendly. It was also

Great Big Sea's biggest market, so even though we didn't have any family on the ground, at least the city wasn't a complete unknown.

I released *You Know I Love You* one track per week over the course of that summer and immediately began to get offers of work from across the country. Most of these requests came from Ontario and, even though we hadn't actually purchased a house in the province yet, I started saying yes and quickly booked myself a solo tour for the fall. House or no house, the show would go on. In the end, we decided to raise our children as Canadians and focused our search on the Ottawa region.

We moved to Manotick, a small village with a great big heart, just twenty-five minutes from downtown Ottawa in August of that year, just in time for the kids to start school. I've heard it said that moving is the most stressful thing you can do in your lifetime (besides dying) and I hope it is something we never have to go through again. These were huge changes for all of us and I am especially proud of how brave my two boys were in facing the challenge. In the end we got lucky and Manotick rewarded us with a relatively soft landing. Newfoundlanders enjoy a well-deserved reputation for friendliness, but I can tell you right now we don't hold a monopoly on being kind. Canada is a friendly country, and I will be forever grateful to the National Capital Region for welcoming my family with open hearts.

I had twenty solo shows booked before I even landed in Ottawa and managed to increase that by another ten before the year was out. I was back to work doing what I loved, and the best part was that I could drive there in my old 2003 Honda Element!

As word spread about my arrival in Ontario, I began to receive invitations to share my story at a variety of mental health and recovery initiatives. I hadn't disclosed my sexual abuse publicly but I had been very open about my recovery, and people were interested in hearing just how the guy from Great Big Sea had been able to stop drinking. The first of these I ever attended was the London Recovery Breakfast in September 2014.

I'd been approached by a speaking agency to participate in the event by talking about my addiction and how music had helped sustain my recovery. I've sung in front of many thousands of people hundreds of times, but

I'd seldom been sober and my words had never had anything to do with truth. I spent days writing and rehearsing a speech with Andrea. I was trying to sound polished and professional. The words were all accurate, but I wasn't feeling 100 percent real when I spoke them out loud. I was only prepared to tell half the story.

On the morning of the event, I was extremely nervous and found myself having to run to the bathroom repeatedly just to look in the mirror and tell myself I was okay. As the hotel ballroom slowly began to fill, I was seated at a table full of strangers and handed an event program. I was to be introduced by a young hockey player named Paulie O'Byrne. I had never heard of Paulie and assumed he was an addict like me and would talk briefly about his own recovery journey before calling me up to the stage. His presentation was brief, just under ten minutes, but the truth he shared in that small period of time was nothing short of enormous. Paulie walked up to the mic and revealed plainly and openly that he'd been sexually assaulted by his hockey coach and how the emotional aftermath of the crime had led him into a life of addiction and despair. His wounds were fresh and I could feel the pain behind his eyes. He had been sober for less than a year. By the time Paulie finished talking, there wasn't a dry eye in the house, including my own. I gave him a hug as he walked past me back to his seat and thanked him for his bravery.

Paulie didn't have a slick, polished PowerPoint presentation. He hadn't used a script or a teleprompter. Paulie had something far more powerful to share that day: he had the truth. When I watched him walk up to that microphone and make himself so vulnerable, I knew I was witnessing real power. Paulie had openly faced his truth in front of five hundred people and survived. More than that, the encounter had visibly made him stronger. His honesty that morning taught me a huge and valuable lesson.

I was so inspired by Paulie's victory that I completely discarded my script, with all its carefully constructed lines. I walked up to that same microphone and defied my own fear. I followed Paulie's example and I just told the truth.

"My name is Séan McCann and I was sexually abused by my priest when I was sixteen...."

The room takes a deep breath in.

"And this is the first time I've ever told anyone...."

The sound of a pin dropping.

"...and it feels so good to let that go."

Tears everywhere.

The truth that had tormented me for over thirty years had finally been released from its prison and I was free from the weight of its chains. I'd stood there in front of five hundred complete strangers and opened myself up from the inside. I'd shown the world my deepest fear, and instead of killing me, it made me stronger. I had walked right through the fire and survived.

My personal revelation was instantly met with intense interest from the press and social media and my phone began to ring just minutes after I left the stage. The first call was from my father. He'd been following the event live on Twitter. We were about to have the conversation I had avoided for my entire life.

He was crying.

"I am so sorry. I had no idea."

I was crying now, too.

"I am too, Dad. I should've done this sooner but I was afraid to hurt you...afraid to hurt me, but I feel so much better now that the truth is out."

"I can't believe I missed this. Can you forgive me?"

"He was a very bad man and he fooled a lot of people. You are a good father and I love you, Dad."

A secret can kill you.

The only way to defeat a secret is to share it.

People drink and use drugs for reasons. I believe in rehabilitation, but we can't solve our problems unless we are first prepared to face them, and that requires real courage. If we do this hard work, we can move forward. We can help ourselves to freedom from addiction and real lives in recovery.

I had booked a show that night in a very small music room called C'est What on Front Street in Toronto. It was my first solo show since revealing my truth, and luckily Andrea had already decided to fly up for the weekend for moral support. She knew I needed her then and she understood that I needed to sing. I have no memory of the show itself, only a feeling of euphoria and release. I let my songs fly like arrows of love and I felt every heart in that tiny room melt together into one. With every song I grew stronger, and for the first time in twenty-five years the stage felt like exactly the place where I was supposed to be. My mask had come off and the people in the audience that night would finally witness the real me as I evolved into the best version of myself. I had faced my truth and would find my way out of the darkness. I had tasted freedom and now I wanted to show others the way. My purpose was made clear. I would try to become a light for the lost. I would help people to help themselves.

ALL IN

♡

WHEN *HELP YOUR SELF* was released in January of 2014, I saw a big breath come out of Séan. Sure he was still stressed and surly, but he was lighter and somewhat happier. The Great Big business was still a shitshow, and he was very angry about how the last tour ended, but he was making his music and telling his story the only way he could at that point, and I was able to see just a little bit of the darkness fade from his eyes.

My constant feeling of not measuring up and being undesirable to Séan, of him not wanting to be in our family, started to lift. It was a feeling I'd struggled with for most of our tumultuous marriage and I've only recently been able to accept that perhaps that's not at all what was going on with Séan all those years. Perhaps he was the one who was feeling inadequate. Perhaps when you measure your worth in units sold and applause or standing ovations, your confidence takes a hit when those sounds fade and the statistics start to diminish. I'm a firm believer that you absolutely can't love someone until you love, or at least forgive and like, yourself. Those are HUGE marching orders for someone steeped in self-loathing and shame.

It's hard to see the forest for the trees when you're actually in the thick of it, trying to hack your way through with your tiny Swiss Army knife. For so long, Séan felt absolutely alone. He was alone in his alcoholism, even on the nights when he had ten thousand people drinking right along with him. He was alone clinging desperately to his secret once he got sober, and, in his mind, he was absolutely alone once he left the band and started from scratch again in the only profession he'd known for twenty-plus years. Of course he couldn't make room in his super-busy head for me and the boys. Well, the boys always, me...I was strong, he figured; I could handle it.

Séan had come such a long way in his sobriety. He was over two years' clean, something I know NO ONE (myself included) had anticipated; he was looking healthier; he was empowered by the music he was putting out and the response he was getting back, and I was so incredibly proud of him. When he was asked to speak at the London Recovery Breakfast in 2014, it was a bit of a shock to both of us. I thought it would be excellent for him, though, however scary, to get up in front of a room of fellow addicts and talk about being an alcoholic in a band (and from a province) known for drinking.

I knew the event was going to be live-tweeted, so I was able to follow along as it was happening. As I was sitting in our house, getting ready to go to the airport to meet Séan in Toronto, the tweets started and I was as nervous for him as I'd ever been. And then this happened:

> 2014-09-26, 9:07 AM
> @itspossibleca: "I don't know if I deserve to be on a stage with these two people" @seanmccannsings says of @Pauline1in5 and Tiffany Rose. #RB2014

> 2014-09-26, 9:09 AM
> POSSIBLE Retweeted
> @CraigGilbert: "My name is @seanmccannsings & I'm an alcoholic." #RB2014

> 2014-09-26, 9:13 AM
> @seanmccannsings puts down his guitar and says "that was the easy part." #RB2014

> 2014-09-26, 9:14 AM
> @itspossibleca: @seanmccannsings says he's never shared this story w/ anyone. Says he can't blame the band for his drinking. More to the story. #RB2014

2014-09-26, 9:19 AM
@itspossibleca: @seanmccannsings says it was an adult from his church when he was a teen that changed his life. Who abused his power, and abused him #RB2014

2014-09-26, 9:20 AM
Addiction Recovery Breakfast London Ontario Retweeted
@CraigGilbert: @seanmccannsings abused by a predator priest. Poured his 1st drink. "Somehow my parents missed that wolf." That wasnt in his notes #RB2014

2014-09-26, 9:20 AM
@itspossibleca: "He destroyed my confidence... He changed my life," @seanmccannsings says. #RB2014

2014-09-26, 9:21 AM
@itspossibleca: @seanmccannsings says he wants to share his story cause "there's more to it than just a guy in a band. There's a guy with heart too." RB2014

2014-09-26, 9:23 AM
@itspossibleca: "I'm a work in progress, honestly," @seanmccannsings tells a packed room at the #ldnont Recovery Breakfast. #RB2014

Holy. Shit.

I was speechless. He'd never actually said those words to me. I knew them, somewhere inside, but he'd never spoken them, and there he was in front of a room full of strangers telling them his truth. Proud doesn't even come close to what I felt at that moment. I was in awe. Shocked. Relieved. Happy? Yeah, I was actually crying. Happily crying for him, for us. I hadn't realized how much weight I was carrying about this. When someone you love is hurting, don't you try to ease the load by taking on some of that emotional weight? I guess I'd done that, because I felt like a piece of dust floating in the air when I read these tweets.

I couldn't get to Séan fast enough. I knew there would be fallout from this admission. I knew the press would pick it up. I knew his parents were definitely going to read about it, if not that day then soon thereafter. It was the second media shitshow in a year for Séan.

THE REST OF 2014 was fraught with coming to terms with Séan's new revelation, more GBS bullshit, and moving. Séan and I felt like a cohesive team for quite possibly the first time in our relationship. We still had fights, we still had bad days, but those bad days never outweighed the good ones. Séan was writing more, spending a couple of weeks in Banff, and finding his new voice in songs that spoke his absolute truth. We took a ten-day vacation to Costa Rica with our new tribe of close friends, and as a family we were beginning to thrive. I knew that whatever else we were going to have to walk through, we'd already walked straight through the fire and survived. I guess you could say it's the year I finally put both feet into the relationship and stopped waiting for Séan to fail in his sobriety. I was all in. Yes, there were dark days, there still are, but I remember telling him during one of those particularly lonely patches that I knew, in the depths of my bones, that his best "work" was yet to come. Truer words I'd never spoken.

I've struggled to communicate my feelings with Séan's parents about his abuse. I love them dearly. They're closer to me than my own parents and more grandparent than either of my children ever knew from my side. They've helped me personally on so many fronts I would never be able to repay them, but with this, I feel they've failed miserably. I've tried to get over how, as a parent, you could put blind trust in any person. I don't. I never have and I never will. But as Séan is quick to point out to me, while raised Catholic, I was not indoctrinated into the Church. I've tried to understand the power and omnipotence of the Church in Newfoundland and in his family, and I'm starting to understand, a little, how this evil human got past them. But when you know better, you do better (thank you, Oprah), and if you're unable to "do" anything about your failure, the least you should do is apologize. Admit your failure. Show you understand the harm your ignorance caused by showing remorse, possibly shame, and eventual acceptance of your shortcomings. I honestly believe it is the only way we get better as humans: admitting our mistakes. We all make them! Admitting them, making reparations if you can, and moving forward with enlightened knowledge is all part of growth, and this is what I wish for Séan and his parents to this day.

I only recently found out about the phone call Séan's dad made to him after the Recovery Breakfast, apologizing. I'm really glad he did that once he heard what had happened. Hearing apologies can be just as healing as speaking your truth.

PART V

REVELATIONS

MENTAL MARKETING

ARMED WITH A renewed sense of purpose, I set out on a mission to change the world and was quickly afforded a multitude of opportunities. My deeply personal revelations and willingness to speak openly about the reasons behind my addiction triggered a series of invitations to participate in a variety of mental health initiatives, and I was eager to join in the fight. Speaking agencies reached out asking for my "exclusive representation" in exchange for financially sustaining and meaningful work. The Twitter followers and Facebook friends who abandoned me when I left the band slowly came back. My phone started to ring again.

I've been a self-employed entrepreneur my entire life in one of the toughest industries on the planet, so I have learned more than a little bit about brand marketing and product exploitation. I know that the easiest way to make money is to give people what they want, even if it's not necessarily good for them...or for you. The artistic concessions we made as a band to sell our brand often left me feeling empty and diluted, and I had no desire to return to that way of doing business. My message as a solo artist and keynote speaker is based entirely on facing personal truth, so I believe it is imperative to preserve its purity moving forward.

It would not take long for my idealism to be put to the test.

The truth is "#mentalhealth" is an industry and it runs on money. Over the past five years, I have learned that far too much of that money is wasted on branding and promotion at the expense of the actual consumer-in-need's well-being. The "product" of mental health has evolved into an extremely popular hashtag for celebrity brands and big corporations to rub up against, because it requires little real effort and it makes those who exploit it appear compassionate and benevolent. Massive online advertising campaigns delivered under the feel-good guise of anti-stigma provide cheap and effective white-collar corporate promotion. The net result is a lot of superficial posturing and mentally unhealthy noise. The whole scene actually reminds me a lot of the music business: all sell with little substance. While advances in public awareness have undeniably been made over the past decade and stigma has been identified and explained, I'd argue that relatively little has improved in the day-to-day life of your average citizen who actually suffers from mental illness and addiction. If we really want to help people, we need to spend far less money on "talk" and a lot more on action.

A good example of this phenomenon is the way Canada treats its veterans. As a country, we allow our politicians to put our soldiers in harm's way and they often return suffering from debilitating physical and mental health issues. PTSD, addiction, and suicide are too often the lifelong side effects for combat survivors. As Canadians we are very proud of our vets, so politicians often exploit them as compelling patriotic speaking points to elicit our votes at election time. They make big promises and they always wear plastic poppies in November. A lot of money is spent in the name of supporting our veterans. Televised Remembrance Day celebrations and Memorial Day parades make for good political capital but, like much else in the mental health world, too much of that cash is spent on branding and not enough actually makes it to the soldiers who need help.

In January 2016, I was invited to speak to the soldiers serving at CFB Petawawa. The Department of Defence was actively promoting a mental health initiative. There had recently been some negative press about PTSD and the military brass wanted the soldiers to know that they were "there for them" and that there would be no negative consequences if they came forward to disclose mental health issues. They set up a press conference on Bell Let's Talk Day led by a major who was also the base psychiatrist. Several hundred enlisted men and women were invited to attend and allowed to ask follow-up questions. This is how the first exchange went:

> Soldier: Did you really mean it when you said that you will be there to help us when we need help with our mental health?

Military Psychiatrist: Absolutely. We are here for you all.
Soldier: I am having some problems, so can I come see you at your clinic?
Military Psychiatrist: Certainly. Just call my office and make an appointment.
Soldier: I tried that, but they told me it would take six months. Can I come see you today? Because I'm suicidal....

In early 2016 I was invited by an organization called Guitars For Vets (G4V) to participate in one of their "Boots On The Ground" walks in Ottawa, during which veterans and volunteers literally comb the downtown core looking for homeless veterans, trying to help them get off the street. I am a pacifist, and up until then I knew very little about how our military worked. Like most Canadians, I assumed that our soldiers were well looked after when they returned from service. Surely we would never let them become homeless? I met with G4V founders Jim and Debbie Lowther and set off towards the ByWard Market armed with coffee coupons, granola bars, basic toiletries, jackets, blankets, and wool socks. It was very cold and it didn't take us long to distribute our supplies as we shivered along the streets of Ottawa.

I encountered an old man sitting outside a pharmacy in a wheelchair smoking a cigarette. It was below zero but he was wearing only a light hoodie and had nothing on his feet. He wasn't a veteran, but I gave him a blanket and some food and asked him where his shoes were. He said that someone had stolen them as he slept, so I offered him some wool socks and helped him pull them on.

Canada is one of the wealthiest nations in the world. Why then are so many of our citizens forced to call a cold cement sidewalk a bed?

We kept walking and eventually found two veterans living on the streets of the ByWard Market. Both were suffering from PTSD and addiction. There are government programs in place for veterans but they are embedded within a complex and confusing bureaucratic process. If you are suffering from addiction or PTSD and looking for help, you will most likely be incapable of navigating the complicated paperwork, and that's one of the reasons why so many veterans continue to fall through the federal cracks. I was deeply moved by the suffering I saw and vowed to help raise money by hosting a benefit concert. I would soon learn exactly how frustrating life as a veteran suffering from mental health issues could be.

Guitars For Vets is a volunteer-run, peer-support-based system bringing veterans together with music. As their website describes, the program "matches veterans and still-serving members with PTSD or other service related disabilities with a gently used guitar and lessons." I believe that music is real and practical medicine because it helped me manage my own mental trauma and addiction, so I saw the sense in this approach and wanted to support it. The then fledgling grassroots program was in huge demand and volunteers were doing their best to keep up. What they really needed were instructors and guitars. I felt that a songwriter's circle would be a great way to promote this cause and an effective way to raise money, so I reached out to my musical friends Joel Plaskett, Jeremy Fisher, and Sarah Harmer, who immediately signed on to help. Tickets would be one hundred dollars (tax-deductible) and every ticket guaranteed a free guitar and ten free lessons for a veteran suffering from mental health problems. This was a really good deal. Unfortunately, that was the end of the easy part. What followed was a long year of frustrating meetings and wasted time.

The bulk of the Canadian military bureaucracy is based in Ottawa, so I assumed we had a built-in audience and the concert would be an easy sell. All we should have had to do was reach out to the military community and spread the word. To that end, I asked my friend Meaghan Smith to design a cool poster to launch the campaign.

The obvious first stop in my mind was the Royal Canadian Legion. Formed in 1925, the mission of this non-profit organization, according to its website, is "to serve Veterans, including serving military and RCMP members and their families, to promote Remembrance, and to serve our communities and our country." G4V sent our poster to the Legion and asked them to share it. We weren't asking for any financial support. All we wanted was for them to share our concert announcement via email and social media to their followers and members. They sent our poster back a week later informing us that the Legion owned the legal copyright and trademark to "the poppy" and that we must immediately remove the flower from our promotion or we could face legal action.

We were definitely not feeling the love from the Legion.

I was shocked, but the vets had heard this story before. The Legion actually does own the legal rights to "the poppy" and has vigorously defended its property in the past. To avoid litigation, we felt it best to remove the offending flower and replace it with the G4V's guitar pick–shaped logo. When we sent the revised image back to the Legion, they still refused to share it. The Legion, they explained, supports a variety of veterans' initiatives and singling us out would be showing favouritism.

This was going to be a lot harder than I thought.

I decided to reach out to Veterans Affairs Canada, whose new minister was actually from my home province of Newfoundland and Labrador. Surely he would help us. After several unanswered emails, I finally coerced his cell number out of a mutual St. John's friend and made a personal call. He listened to my pitch and promised to do everything he could to help promote the event.

He dropped two tweets the week before the event. He didn't come to the show.

Next stop, the Department of National Defence. I attended two separate meetings with the deputy minister who, both times, pledged her support. Again, the target here was not financial. We weren't coming in with our hands out, looking for a cheque. All we asked was for the department to share our promotional materials with the military community on their extensive social media networks. The deputy minister asked me to come to DND headquarters to speak and sing for the staff during their annual mental health awareness day and I agreed. I thought it might be a good opportunity to finally get the word out. I freely shared my story and sang my heart out and I met some really good people that day. We had a booth set up to sell tickets to the concert.

We sold two.

A week later we were informed that, while the department could allow the poster to be viewed in its offices, its policies forbade them from sharing our promotional materials in any other official way.

For fuck sakes.

In a last-ditch effort to gain even a little political support, the G4V team asked me to bring Old Brown to Parliament Hill where we would host an awareness event in a room right outside the House of Commons doors. I ended up singing for a dozen people. We sold another six tickets.

It was now one month out from the event and we had sold fewer than two hundred of the seven hundred potential tickets. We had done everything we could think of to engage the extensive local military community and failed to secure any meaningful support. I couldn't believe this was actually happening. I thought for sure this show would sell itself to a built-in local, sympathetic audience. I was wrong. It was now time to take the campaign to the civilian population by engaging local media. If we couldn't sell the cause, we could still sell the concert. I immediately started making local television and radio appearances and calling in personal favours.

In the end, we sold just under six hundred tickets and raised fifty thousand dollars to pay for free guitars and lessons for hundreds of veterans in crisis. The show was singularly incredible and those in the audience could tell they were witnessing something really special. I will be forever grateful to Joel and Jeremy and Sarah for lending their time and voices to this worthy cause.

I learned a lot from this experience, not least of which was how little real and practical support our veterans actually receive from the very people elected and charged with looking after their well-being. I can honestly say that I have never worked so hard in my life to sell a show. I was surprised and disappointed on many levels, but I didn't give up because I really believe that our veterans deserve better. As Canadians, we all do.

By the end of my second year as a "mental health advocate," I had accumulated so many corporate logos I began to feel like a NASCAR driver. The mental health racetrack was so littered with useless catchphrases and promotional debris, I lost sight of the finish line and began to feel like I was spinning my wheels.

And then I met Sheldon Kennedy.

A former NHL player and fellow survivor of both addiction and sexual abuse, Sheldon and I were cut from the same cloth. We hit it off immediately over too much coffee and carrot cake in the ByWard Market in early 2016. Two years younger than me, but a twenty-year veteran of the Canadian mental health scene, Sheldon understood my frustration and helped me navigate the complex corporate world of mental health marketing. Instead of letting his message be co-opted, Sheldon managed to cut through all the noise and focus his truth where it could have a real and lasting impact on people in need. With his business partner, Wayne McNeil, Sheldon successfully lobbied federal and provincial governments to make long-overdue changes in laws regarding child sexual abuse, and in 2013 they opened the Sheldon Kennedy Child Advocacy Centre in Calgary. This was more than just political posturing and corporate happy-speak. These were real accomplishments and practical results. The centre's name was changed, at Kennedy's request, in 2018 and is now the Calgary & Area Child Advocacy Centre. According to CBC News, Kennedy believed having his name associated with the building suggested he would "take responsibility for its day-to-day operation," which had taken an emotional toll on him. He is an incredible example of how you must help yourself first if you're ever going to be help anyone else.

There's just no bullshit with Sheldon, and in the industry of #mentalhealth this is a rare and refreshing thing to behold. Sheldon is more than just a mentor; he's my brother and my friend, and together there's not enough carrot cake in the world to keep us down.

If Sheldon Kennedy is my brother in arms, then Clara Hughes is most certainly my warrior sister. Armed with the conviction and the strength of an Olympian, Clara is a physical and mental force to be reckoned with. Her courage in openly fighting her battle with depression challenged social stigmas and inspired millions to speak up and ultimately help themselves. She, too, is a brave, no-bullshit individual who is unafraid to really be herself in every circumstance. In a field filled with phonies and false prophets, Clara Hughes is always the real fucking deal. Where I find medicine in music, Clara seeks solace in movement to maintain a balanced and healthy body and mind. Unfortunately for me, this often takes the form of long and arduous hikes up and down the Canadian Rocky Mountains, which is how we prefer to spend our time together. My very first mountain summit was shared with Clara and the experience left me with sore legs and a head full of clear blue sky. My road to recovery has been fraught with many twists and turns, but every step I've ever taken in the company of Clara Hughes has led me upwards. When we're together, I feel like we can move mountains.

Early in my sobriety a wise old reformed alcoholic told me that while recovery might cost me some relationships, I would eventually find "better friends ahead," and his words of encouragement have proven to be correct. I used to be surrounded by hundreds of shallow acquaintances but now I can count my real friends on two hands. I would rather have a single true companion than a hundred false friends, and I am grateful to Sheldon and Clara for showing me the difference.

YOU KNOW
I LOVE YOU

GREAT BIG SEA did not end well and I take fully one-third of the responsibility for that failure. My decision to be on the bus sober caused a serious increase in tension, and in retrospect I should probably never have boarded. You may have heard this analogy before, and I can assure you that it holds true: being in a band is like being in a marriage—a very cold and loveless marriage that goes on for way too long...between three dudes. Leaving a band is very much like going through a divorce, and arguably just as painful, and this was not a decision I made lightly. We always made really good money and I still had a family to support, but I needed to move away from a very unhealthy lifestyle in order to get better. In order to survive. Money has never brought out the best in anybody, and in the end we decided that an unemployed Dad is better than a dead one. Unfortunately, as in many divorces, our views on a "fair settlement" were radically different and I became very frustrated...and angry.

At the end of the summer of 2014, the small town of Burlington, Newfoundland, invited me to take part in their annual Gathering Festival. I was suspicious that they might be expecting to score some Great Big Sea for cheap so I informed the committee I was no longer singing any GBS songs if that was what they were looking for. They reassured me that I could sing whatever I wanted and suggested I just come out and relax. Truth is, at that time I really only knew GBS songs, so when I got there I found myself walking around the woods backstage trying to think of something else to sing, when all of a sudden I encountered a woman crawling around on the ground. I thought she must have fallen and asked:

"Are you okay?"

"Yes, I'm fine."

"What are you doing?"

"Looking for a four-leaf clover."

"Do you ever find any?"

"Yes...all the time."

Then she went on:

"I know you...you're Séan McCann, and I came here to tell you something. You must never give up!"

"Oh really...."

"Yes, really.

"My name is Anne-Lise Boyer and I am from Fergus, Ontario, and I'm a huge GBS fan. I have gone to many of your concerts, but ten years ago I was hit by a drunk driver and I have a brain injury, which is why I speak so directly. I haven't been able to go to a concert in ten years because the lights and the volume cause me to have seizures. I drove all the way from Ontario to hear you sing because I knew this festival would not be too loud or flashy...and to tell you that your music really matters and that you must NEVER GIVE UP."

I was floored.

"So will you be singing any GBS songs tonight...?"

My heart almost burst.

"I will now."

It was my second moment of clarity. A switch had flipped and that night I sang only GBS songs and I felt a huge weight lift off my shoulders. A feeling of peace came over me as I let go of more and more anger with every verse. After the set, Anne-Lise came up and gave me a great big hug—and then she gave me the four-leaf clover she'd found on the ground right before the show. I had the flower encased in silver and I wear it every day to help me remember how lucky I truly am.

The sad truth is that I'm pretty sure my former, alcoholic self would not have bothered to ask, "Are you okay?"

I was far too self-absorbed to care, and I paid people to protect me from the outside world. To keep me in my dark cocoon and prevent any real light from getting in. I realize now that my addiction must have caused me to miss out on a great many beautiful experiences over the past thirty-five years.

I am grateful that I was awake and present enough not to miss this one. I had opened up my heart and let a stranger in and the simple lesson she taught me changed my life forever.

Anger is the enemy.

It never wants to help or heal...only hurt.

ANGER can only be defeated by LOVE.

Anne-Lise still struggles every day with her injury but she never gives up. We stay in touch and her inspirational emails always seem to show up on the days when I need them most. She is still finding four-leaf clovers.

🍀

A REPORTER RECENTLY asked me if I was concerned that my sons would eventually find out about my history. She was shocked when I told her they already knew. I have faced my truth. My past is no longer my prison and I will never again be forced to live in fear. I have helped myself and I am no longer a Victim.

I am a Survivor.

I consider my sobriety to be my greatest accomplishment and I am very proud of myself and I know my children are extremely proud of their father, because I chose them over alcohol and they know I did it because I love them. I want my boys to know that their dad does not hide from his problems. I want to teach them how to be brave so they will be able to overcome their own fears when they inevitably come.

Because I love them more than anything.

You Know / Love You

You know I love you
 You know I care
You know I miss you
 When I'm not there

I carry you with me
Everywhere I go
 Because I love you
And now you know
I've climbed the mountains
I've crossed the sea

The lonesome valleys
And the grand prairie

I carry you with me
For all to see
Because I love you
You can count on me
I've done so many miles alone
I've learned some things I should've known

I let myself get led off track
But you keep me coming back
You know I love you, you know I care
You know I miss you, when I'm not there

I carry you with me
Everywhere I roam

Because I love you

I am not alone

ADDICTION GOES DIGITAL

"Hi, my name is Séan and I'm an alcoholic...."

THIS IS HOW I begin every sharing session with my brothers and sisters struggling to stay sober in detox centres. I do this work pro bono because I have compassion for anyone who struggles with addiction. I have seen first-hand the damage this disease can inflict on a person and on the people around them. Homes broken, families torn apart, entire lives left unlived. I have personally lost many friends who eventually succumbed to the habits they were ultimately unable to break. Without recovery, there is only destruction and death.

"Addiction" can be very simply defined as behaviour we cannot control in spite of its harmful consequences. According to Statistics Canada, roughly 5.8 million Canadians aged 12 or older self-report as heavy drinkers. Approximately 6 million Canadians (21 percent of our current population) will suffer from some form of addiction in their lifetime, and alcohol is by far the main culprit at 19 percent. I've been an alcoholic for almost thirty-five years, so I know exactly how much damage addiction can do and how hard it is to overcome.

As I write this I am fifty-two years old, which means I was born almost twenty-five years before the internet was invented. I was thirty-two when I received my first email and forty-one when I fired off my first tweet. It was 2008 before I bought a BlackBerry and learned how to type with my thumbs. I've lived more than half of my life without the seductive glow of artificial light that flows from the millions of screens we now face daily.

Times have changed.

My two boys, Keegan, now fourteen, and Finnegan, eleven, were raised on screens. The iPad was by far their favourite babysitter and "Hey, Google" is now one of their most commonly used phrases. Currently their community playground is the extremely popular online video game Fortnite. This is where they meet their friends to socialize while, unfortunately, firing digital bullets at each other. Their casual conversation is peppered with references to "kills" and "snipes" and an entire fan-based celebrity culture has grown up around the game. When they aren't allowed to play, they watch their heroes do it for them on YouTube. Gamers are the new rock stars. Space Invaders is the only video game I ever played, so I am having a hard time keeping up with all these new goings on and have come to accept the derogative descriptor, Boomer. While I fail to see the fascination, I do see some disturbing patterns in my kids' behaviour:

1. They will say and do just about anything to get our permission to play the game.
2. Once they start playing, they are incapable of stopping.

On more than one occasion, my children have even gone so far as to tell me they are not playing when they are actively engaged in the pursuit right in front of my eyes. This, of course, constitutes another clear and common sign of dependence: denial.

These behaviours, to me, demonstrate typical symptoms of addiction, so I began to wonder if my kids required some kind of intervention. To test this theory, Andrea decided to let the boys play the game freely one Saturday without any parental control or interference, just to see how long they would go before stopping on their own. They crawled up out of the rec room seven hours later—hungry, bleary-eyed, dehydrated, and extremely SURLY. I don't think Keegan had even been to the washroom. We were unwittingly raising two video game vampires.

While it remains a constant battle, we can still exert some control over how much time the boys spend online while they are in the house. Neither of us has any problem being the "fun police," but unfortunately our practical jurisdiction ends at the driveway, as both our boys are equipped with the latest smartphone devices. We like this because, in theory, it allows them to take us with them wherever they go, but I feel like they are also literally carrying "god" around in their pockets. Her new name is Siri and she knows the answer to just about every question you can think of...even if you shouldn't. Like it or not, this is the world we live in, and as parents we are forced to adapt or—like last year's iPhone—become obsolete.

If gaming is addictive in the same way as coffee or cigarettes, then social media must be the chronic equivalent of crack cocaine. Where else can we chase a dopamine rush with a flick of a fingertip, our hearts and egos bursting just a little bit with every "friend" and "follower" we actively solicit? Our personal worth is increasingly measured in terms of "likes" as we expose ourselves to instant world judgement with every post we release. The pressure to be perfect pushes people to manipulate and present distorted versions of their true selves. Genuine identity is lost—or even worse, deliberately suppressed. To make matters worse, behind every screen there hides a thousand highly trained software engineers whose sole purpose is to find more compelling ways to keep your eyes and thumbs on that screen. Data is the world's most valuable new commodity and our social media masters are now addicting us deliberately...for money.

It must really SUCK to be a teenager today.

While clinical studies of digital addiction or "Internet addiction disorder" (IAD) are really just getting started, I am forging ahead with two very controversial and experimental intervention techniques on my own children:

1. Walking outside in the fresh air.
2. Talking to each other face to face.

So far the results have been very positive. My boys know how to look people in the eyes when they say hello, and that they are worth much more than the sum of their "likes."

The digital age came on fast and strong and I feel like society is struggling to keep up with the negative side effects brought on by relentless technological advances. We are in the middle of a massive social revolution and it's playing out daily across our screens. Fake news infects the internet and truth has become a moving target. Foreign countries interfere with democratic elections and presidents incite division and fear. Point-and-shoot entertainment desensitizes against violence and mass murderers broadcast their crimes on Facebook in real time. Attention spans fractured by constant distraction cripple dinner conversations. Everything is happening everywhere, to everyone, all the time.

There is nowhere left to hide.

I remember landing at Toronto's Pearson International Airport about five years ago. I had an hour layover between flights and was slowly meandering around the busy terminal looking for a place to sit down. There must've been between two and three thousand people there, so I ended up having to stand. As I was leaning in a corner, scanning my various social media for entertainment, I slowly became aware of something very strange. As crowded as the terminal was, I didn't hear a sound. Nobody was talking. Everyone I could see was looking at a little screen, just like me. Lost in our own digital bubbles, completely oblivious to the human beings living and breathing right next to us. Especially the children. We were all fully connected on one level but completely disconnected on another. I stopped my surfing and started to take a long, slow look around. I saw faces from just about every race, creed, age, and colour standing there in one room together, but completely separate and alone. The one thing I couldn't see were people's eyes, because they were all looking down.

Devices can be DIVISIVE.

Social media's promise of connection has proven to be superficial and false, delivering us instead straight into the arms of isolation. Modern technology has given us a great many gifts, but it will never be able to show us any real compassion. How to love. To laugh. To cry.

I have spent the last five years criss-crossing the country and sharing my truth with people in small halls and theatres, face to face. I do it because I believe there is a beneficial exchange of real and positive power when people gather together physically to sing and to share. Singing a song can open up a heart and relieve its sorrow, and a burden shared makes for a lighter load.

People often ask me how I continue to remain sober. What is my method?

Do I follow the 12 steps? Do I go to Alcoholics Anonymous meetings? Am I in therapy? I have tried all of these things and learned a little from them all, but none was strong enough to maintain my recovery. Music is the only medicine that ever really worked for me. The truth is, I keep doing these concerts and speaking events because they give me the opportunity to make myself vulnerable, and I believe there is great power in that. When I am onstage, alone and exposed, armed with nothing but the truth and a guitar, I always find the best version of myself that I can be. The strong me. The honest me. The compassionate me. The real me.

Addiction, be it chemical, alcohol, or digital, is always an attempt to hide from truth and to avoid pain. It is a liar and a thief and a prison for our true potential. As a father, I want to teach my children how to be open and honest and brave. I want to give them the tools they need to face their problems and the skills they require to make good decisions. I want to show them how to walk confidently through this life with their eyes facing forward and looking up.

Freely and without fear.

LITTLE MISS KNOW-IT-ALL

♡

ALTHOUGH I'VE LIVED with two in my lifetime, I will never profess to know how to get through life with an alcoholic. And though I've managed to come through it, I'll never suggest to anyone how they might make a worthwhile life, even when they feel eclipsed daily by the brightness of their partner, or their family's overbearing ways. I'm not a doctor. I'm not a therapist. I am a mother of two boys with a political science degree, that's it. But I know perseverance. I know loyalty. I know love. I know pain and joy and everything in between. And most of all I know that facing all the shit you don't want to face will inevitably end in something better than what you started with. It won't be pretty and it won't be easy. You'll want to quit, and quite possibly may quit more than once, but if you can pick yourself back up and just keep moving forward, even an inch at a time, you will get there. I know that we, ALL OF US, are WAY stronger than we ever believe ourselves to be. Yes, pain is horrible, but you are stronger than that pain, you just have to be willing to feel it, breathe it in, and RELEASE it.

Séan and I still have (very) difficult days. There are times when I want nothing more than to walk away from his loudness and all of his baggage, and I'm certain he feels the same about me. But we stay. We fight for us. We fight for ourselves, for each other, for us as a couple, and for us as a family.

I remember watching a documentary with Séan one night in 2015 as we were going through a particularly bad patch. It was called *George Harrison: Living in the Material World*, and in it, George Harrison's wife, Olivia, was asked by the interviewer how, in the wake of George's non-belief in the "ownership" of things, including partners and spouses, they stayed married for all those years. Her response has stuck with me; she said, "You just don't get divorced." I was stymied. Yes. You STAY. I've taken that to heart, especially in all those times when walking away would be easier.

Please don't misunderstand me: Séan and I are like you. We have our problems. We are still fighting our demons daily. However, I have come to believe, and it has been continually proven to me over time, that the sum of us is far greater and more powerful in this world than our individual selves.

I have also learned to recognize what I need. I need people. I need a tribe, and I need to know I'm not walking this path alone. I have that in Séan, yes, but I also need it in others, and realizing that Séan and I aren't the only people trying to find their way through tragedy and adversity was an amazing revelation. I know you have a story. I know you might be feeling alone. I can tell you with absolute certainty in my heart that you are NOT alone.

You. Are. Not. Alone.

You are worthy of love. Do not give up on yourself. Because above everything else I've learned through this tumultuous journey, we are all very much worth fighting for and we are definitely worthy of love.

MUSIC IS MY RELIGION

FAITH HAS BEEN around for as long as there have been questions beyond our human capacity to answer.

Why are we here?

Why do we have to die?

Where do we go when we do?

For millennia our finest thinkers have wrestled with these fundamental questions but have always fallen short of finding any real, concrete answers. Where science fails, religion flourishes by providing the answers we so desperately crave, without any burden of actual proof. Religious belief depends entirely upon the surrender of reason to a divine higher power, a price that billions are prepared to pay instead of living daily with the dreaded alternative: the great unknown.

I was baptized into the Catholic faith when I was just four days old. In a room full of witnesses and with the full blessing of my parents, a priest held my tiny head under cold water and claimed my immortal soul forever. It was an eternal life commitment made without my consent and I was helpless to stop it. My tears were the only protest I could offer. Like the rest of my extended family for generations, I was raised under the rules of the church and taught to accept its teachings unconditionally. I believed in Jesus and Mary and Joseph. I believed in God, the Father, and the Holy Spirit. I believed in heaven and hell, angels and demons, sinners and saints. I believed in it all. Not because I chose to, but because I was told to.

I was a good Catholic. I went to confession every Friday and mass every Sunday. I still know all the Eucharistic responses and the mysteries of the rosary off by heart. I remember every station of the cross and all

three forms of the Act of Contrition (traditional, simplified, and modern).
I accepted and memorized it all without question or reservation.

I was born to believe.

I still remember, word for word, my first confession to the priest who
would sexually abuse me. Before he absolved me, I tried to impress him
by reciting the longer, traditional Act of Contrition:

> O my God, I am heartily sorry for having offended thee,
> and I detest all my sins because of Thy just punishment.
> Most of all because they offend my God,
> who art all-good and deserving of all my love.
> I firmly resolve, with the help of Thy grace,
> to sin no more,
> and to avoid the near occasion of sin.
> Amen.

I *liked* that the priest had taken an interest in me and I wanted to
keep his attention and remain in his favour. I *liked* having a priest for a
best friend. It made me feel special and privileged and cool. I *liked* driving
around in his car late at night. I *liked* drinking his wine and firing his illegal
rifle. I enjoyed almost everything about our relationship...until I didn't.
When I look back now on all that went wrong, the thing that hurts me the
most is the fact that I liked him. So. Fucking. Much.

I may no longer have faith in organized religion but I do accept our
human spirituality, and here is what I've come to believe: indoctrination
is a very dangerous practice because it robs us of our instinctive rational
defenses and offers evil people an advantage they will inevitably exploit.
It shelters the wicked by clouding otherwise capable minds, and makes
innocent children vulnerable to harm. My mom and dad were decent people and good parents and I bet they inherited those traits from their own
mothers and fathers. Unfortunately, they also inherited the ancient DNA of
a highly profitable and well-branded, professional, organized religion that
promised to remove all doubt from their spiritual lives for the small price
of a few souls. After centuries of systemic indoctrination, my family was

so intergenerationally traumatized by the same church that had sworn to protect us that we were powerless to fend off the physical and emotional attacks of its ordained priest.

Religion has been either the underlying cause or a major contributor to most of the wars in the history of this world. Its only rival for first place in that disreputable regard is money. One would think, given the potentially dangerous consequences, that choosing any religion should be a purely personal and fully informed decision, made only when someone is mature enough to think for him- or herself. The Catholic Church is one of the richest financial institutions on the planet, with the Vatican alone believed have an estimated net worth of between $10 and $15 billion USD (not including its enormous collection of priceless art). Instead of using its vast wealth to help its victims of sexual violence, the Church holds itself above the law and continues to hide its pedophile priests.

In 1998 my own abuser was accused again, in England, of trying to abduct young boys with his car while posing as an American tourist in Oxford. In an article published in 2001 in a number of UK papers, including the *Guardian* and the *Telegraph,* he was said to have been sentenced to "three years' probation with regular psychiatric treatment." He admitted he had been "suffering from a deep-seated anger about his strict upbringing and wanted to take it out on the boys." Instead of facing any meaningful consequences and despite his previous legal record from Newfoundland, the priest was moved again to a new parish, where he continues to hear confessions and say mass to this day.

🍀

AT THE VATICAN SUMMIT which took place from February 21 to 24, 2019, and was suppoesd to finally address the crisis of sexual abuse of minors by clergy, Pope Francis was unable to commit to a policy of zero tolerance for child sexual abuse among the clergy. Child sexual abuse is immoral and illegal. Is zero tolerance really too much for the world's 1.2 billion Catholics to expect of its priests? Can anyone still believe that a man who would say something so wrong is really infallible? The Church may lay claim to divine impunity in heaven, but shouldn't it be held legally accountable for the laws it breaks here on earth?

Every month or so there seems to be a new scandal involving the sexual abuse of children by clergy. Boston, MA; Pennsylvania, PA; Washington, DC; Perth, AU; St. John's, NL. When will we finally see the end of these heinous crimes and the lifelong impacts they leave behind in survivors? After all that has been revealed, I fail to comprehend how any person who has a legitimate spiritual calling could ever seriously consider working for an institution as morally corrupt as the Catholic Church.

In spite of everything that's happened I still consider myself to be a spiritual person, but I believe faith is something an individual should choose rather than be baptised into. Indoctrination from birth impairs our children's ability to recognize imminent danger and obstructs our parental duty to protect. While I don't accept the beliefs of any of the world's organized religions, I do believe in acceptance. I even learned a new prayer that has proven very helpful over the past nine years. I find myself referring to it often...I just leave out the "God" bit:

Grant me the serenity to accept the things I cannot change.

I was sexually abused by my parish priest when I was a teenager.

The courage to change the things I can.

I am an alcoholic but I do not drink.

And the wisdom to know the difference.

I can move forward with confidence because my decisions will be made with a clear and sober mind. This world can be a very difficult and dangerous place and I understand the temptation to surrender, rather than confront its many challenges. I have learned from experience that our problems cannot be solved unless we are first prepared to face them.

Our faith is not something we should invest blindly into a religious corporation. If the promise of religion is to help us navigate life's many tragedies and mysteries, then the religion I choose is music. I write songs to help me understand what happens beyond my control and I sing them to celebrate my very survival. Isn't that what religion is supposed to do? If so, then music is my religion because it brings us together and makes us stronger. It comes from nowhere and everywhere and it lives in each and every one of us. If that isn't God, then I don't know what is.

I believe that evil exists because I have seen it with my own eyes, and I believe in the goodness of people because I can hear it when we sing together. I can't explain this but I believe it to be true. Faith is something we must learn to put more in each other if the human race is going to survive. Real faith is not about money or power or judgment or rules. Real faith is about love, and this world needs that today more than ever.

We are made of more than blood and bone.

We are made of music and we are made of love.

This Life is an Ocean of Love

A river runs slow
Deeply and low
Steady but never still
Like leaves in the wind
We shiver and spin
Blown without a will

A man walks alone
A long way from home
Far from his family and friends
Like a blackbird he flies
Across darkening skies
Trying to get back to them

On and on and on and on
We whistle at the sun
On and on and on and on
We run

A baby is born
Like a thunderstorm
A father's pride lights up the night
In the wink of an eye,
A lifetime goes by
One chance to get it right

This life is an ocean of love
Let every heart rise above

POSTSCRIPT

YOU'RE PROBABLY WONDERING why I haven't brought formal charges against the priest who assaulted me. I have considered my legal options several times since sobering up and accepting what happened to me, but the truth is I just don't trust the justice system or the Catholic Church to do the right thing. In Newfoundland, this predator was caught with his hands quite literally on the smoking gun (and the steering wheel), but the law failed to prosecute him and protect the general public. He was instead shuffled off to England, where he was hauled in again for attempted malfeasance with minors, only to be let go once more without consequence. The Catholic Church has done an excellent job of protecting its many ordained pedophiles while the international justice system has consistently failed to defend and support millions of victims of sexual abuse. After thirty-five years of suffering in silence I am finally willing to share my truth, but I refuse to re-victimize myself or drag my family through a long public trial that will never bring us any real satisfaction or peace. I will place my faith in the laws of Karma and trust that, in the end, we all shall reap what we sow.

The purpose of this book is not to exact vengeance.

We wrote this for the many who remain lost and have yet to realize they are not alone. We wrote this for those who suffer from secrets, so they might gain the courage to face their own truth and move forward with their lives. We wrote this so the many laid low by addiction might learn that recovery is always possible. We wrote this for our children, so they may see the world with open eyes and still walk fearlessly through it.

But most of all we wrote this for ourselves.

This is our love story.

This is our life.

ACKNOWLEDGEMENTS

Keegan and Finnegan for being the two best boys ever.

Matt Wells for careful input, constant encouragement, and being a perpetual sounding board.

Jamie Aragon for all things too numerous to even mention, but mostly your unwavering stoic strength and love.

Steve, Anne Marie and Samantha Philip for being excellent neighbours and even better family.

Clara Hughes and Sheldon Kennedy for their unwavering support and showing me that I am not alone.

Joel Plaskett and Jeremy Fisher for being great musical collaborators and even better friends.

Chris Murphy for playing Sancho to my Don.

Jennie Stamm for knowing the rest of the stories not told and still loving me anyway.

Anne Lise Boyer for teaching me how to never give up.

Paulie O'Byrne for showing me how to be brave enough to face my truth.

Betsy, Julie and Terri, my small but very mighty Tribe, who picked me up, dusted me off and forced me to laugh at everything (don't worry, our book is next).

Easter Seals NL for teaching me how to sing with an open heart again.

Julie Swatosch for coming when I called and hearing my cry for help.

All the animals who drew love out of our hearts even when we had none to show each other: Kitty, Tosh, Marley, Storm, Ashes, Karma and Bodhi.

Old Brown for being a friend to me when I really needed one but there were none to be found.

Tamara Ross and Banff Centre for enabling me to be fearlessly alone.

Ted Rowe for his archival assistance.

Steven Pasternak who would prefer to remain nameless.

Whitney Moran for organizing our thoughts into readable sentences and believing in our two voices from the beginning.

Sarah Miniaci for reading our book and helping us promote it anyway.

SONGWRITING CREDITS

FIRE © Séan McCann, David Matheson, Joel Plaskett

HOLD ME MOTHER © Séan McCann, Joel Plaskett

STONE COLD HEART © Séan McCann, Paul Lamb

RED WINE and WHISKEY © Séan McCann, Joel Plaskett

LONG ROAD LEAD ME ON © Séan McCann

RAZOR and RUST © Séan McCann, Jeen O'Brien

DOIN' FINE © Séan McCann, Paul Lamb

ONE GOOD REASON © Séan McCann, Paul Lamb

STRONGER © Séan McCann

THE SINGER WHO LOST HIS SONG © Séan McCann

GOODBYE OLD FRIEND © Séan McCann

TAKE OFF MY ARMOUR © Séan McCann

YOU KNOW I LOVE YOU © Séan McCann

THIS LIFE (IS AN OCEAN OF LOVE) © Séan McCann

MY SECRET

If you have something that is too hard to say, then write it down here.